MW00451195

THE
613TH
COMMANDMENT

January 17, 1983

Rabbi Jacob Simcha Cohen
Congregation Shaarei Tefila
7269 Beverly Blvd.
Los Angeles, CA 90036

Dear Rabbi Cohen Shlita,

It was considerate of you to permit me to see your
sefer while still in manuscript.

I consider your sefer a remarkable achievement. It
presents in the English language the full flavor of
"talking in learning". You have made it possible for
those limited to English to be able to follow the
flow of Talmudic reasoning involved in elucidating a
"Sugya" - a talmudic discourse.

At the same time the sefer makes available the
clarification in lucid terms of complex concepts that
will expand the Torah horizon of all who learn it.

בברכת כט״ס, בידידות ומכבדו

יעקב שמשון וינברג

Rabbi Yaakov S. Weinberg
Rosh HaYeshiva
Ner Israel, Baltimore, Maryland
Kerem, Santa Clara, California

THE
613TH
COMMANDMENT

An Analysis
of the *Mitzvah*
to Write a *Sefer Torah*
(Derush VeChiddush)

J. Simcha Cohen

JASON ARONSON, INC.
Northvale, New Jersey
London

10 9 8 7 6 5 4 3 2 1

Library of Congress Cataloging-in-Publication Data

Cohen, J. Simcha.
   The 613th commandment : an analysis of the *mitzvah* to write
a *sefer torah (Derush VeChiddush)* / J. Simcha Cohen.
      p.   cm.
   Previously published: New York : Ktav, c 1983.
   Includes index.
   ISBN 1-56821-249-6
   1. Torah scrolls (Jewish law) 2. Scribes, Jewish. I. Title.
II. Title: Six hundred thirteenth commandment.
BM657.T6C63   1994
296.4–dc20
                                                            94-9226

Manufactured in the United States of America. Jason Aronson Inc. offers books and cassettes. For information and catalog write to Jason Aronson Inc., 230 Livingston Street, Northvale, New Jersey 07647.

Dedicated To
Abisch and Esther Nagel (z″l),
whose loving memory was
sanctified
by a *Sefer Torah*
expressly written in their behalf
by their children
Jack and Gitta Nagel
and grandchildren
Ronald (Cheryl),
Esther (Paul),
David (Wendy),
Careena (Drew),
and great-grandchildren.

Contents

Introduction

The *Sefer Torah* is one of the most prized possessions of the Jew. It commands great respect and reverence and is afforded a degree of *kedushah* not matched by any other ritual object. Its function and importance are quite well known, even to those with minimal Jewish knowledge. Indeed, it symbolizes the uniqueness of our religious values and the *raison d'être* of our culture.

Tradition has it that there are 613 *mitzvot* in the Torah, all of which are incumbent upon the observant Jew. Among the 613 *mitzvot* is the commandment to actually write one's own copy of the *Sefer Torah*. In our day, observance of this *mitzvah* is a rare phenomenon. The high cost factor is prohibitive, limiting the number of practitioners. Moreover, since *Sifrei Torah* are generally available, many view the *mitzvah* as a luxury rather than a necessity. As a result, the *mitzvah* is hardly ever observed, and to compound the problem, many people do not have adequate knowledge of the *mitzvah*. Even *yeshivot* do not study the laws of this *mitzvah* in any depth.

The original discourses in this book are presented in an attempt to heighten general awareness of this neglected *mitzvah*. The medium of the English language is utilized to enable the vast number of Jews who are either unable or unwilling to read such material in Hebrew to be involved in the process of learning about this *mitzvah*. Indeed, the process itself is an experiment, based upon my long-standing view that many Jews are interested in acquiring Torah knowledge but lack the technical ability to comprehend Talmudic and Halachic texts in Hebrew.

In writing this book, as a means of underscoring the nature of the material presented, I have adopted as my format the analytic approach of traditional rabbinic responsa literature rather than that of secular research. The discourses in the pages that follow, concentrating upon specific concepts related to the purpose of the *mitzvah* of writing a *Sefer Torah*, comprise an original Torah analysis in English, not an academic research project, and in this sense may be viewed as exemplifying a form of modern-day *pilpul*. Indeed, the ideas presented are in the tradition of a *sheur*, and the positions delineated are not to be regarded as definitive Halachah. It is my hope that these discourses will engender questions, debate, and dialogue, as well as an acute sensitivity to a neglected *mitzvah*. For those who are not familiar with the traditional forms of Jewish scholarship, they will also serve as an introduction to the methodology of Torah creativity.

Two recent converging factors crystallized my serious personal interest in the neglected *mitzvah* of writing a *Sefer Torah*. The first, of course, was the active role of the Lubavitcher Rebbe, *Shlita*. The Rebbe not only publicly emphasized the importance of this *mitzvah*, but embarked upon a far-reaching campaign to unify Jewish children throughout the world by enabling them to acquire letters in a holy *Sefer Torah* written exclusively in their behalf.

This campaign generated intense excitement about the *mitzvah*. In every major city, and certainly in Los Angeles, young Chasidim visit synagogues and even stand on street corners to promulgate the importance of personal involvement with a *Sefer Torah*.

Simultaneously, Jack Nagel, a noted national leader and former president of Congregation Shaarei Tefila, Los Angeles, California, informed me of his family's decision to have a *Sefer Torah* written expressly in memory of his beloved parents, Abisch and Esther Nagel, *zichronan livrachah*. He also requested an opportunity to learn the laws and sources of this *mitzvah* which he so cherished. I saw this as an opportunity to stimulate active and serious study into the scope of a *mitzvah* which I was truly concerned about. As a result, a special *sheur* was implemented, attended regularly by Mr. Nagel and his son, David. A great part of the Torah analysis herein presented was developed during the course of this *sheur* and the preparation for it. Thus, many of the thoughts that I elaborate in this book are truly intertwined in the fabric of the unique *Sefer Torah* presented by the Nagel family to Congregation Shaarei Tefila in Adar 5742 (1982).

As I wrote the various chapters, I circulated them amongst a number of *Rabbanim, Roshëi Yeshivah* and *B'nai Torah*. In addition, I used the *Chiddushei Torah* as the basis for a series of public *sheurim* at Congregation Shaarei Tefila. My concern was to establish a dialogue on Torah concepts, for Torah is the one vehicle that penetrates all barriers to communication. No matter what their age, cultural attainments, country of origin, or *yeshivah* background, Torah is the equalizer of all Jews. It is the language of our people and the medium that interweaves the past with the future. This process opened channels for a most enjoyable interchange of ideas and critical thoughts.

All who study Torah with true sensitivity share the view that it is an exciting venture into the realm of ideas. Each concept in Torah is related to another and yet another. The more one learns, the more one is stimulated to seek further knowledge and clarity. The learning process dramatically and vividly crystallizes the grand, masterful scholarship of our sages as well as the obvious limitations of our own abilities. Thus, it is through intense study of Torah that one begins to appreciate somewhat the adage that "Torah is life."

Throughout this process my beloved Rebbitzen, Shoshana, has encouraged my efforts. It is because of her gentle patience, deep understanding, and high regard for Torah that I was able to devote energy and thought to intense Torah scholarship. Her *zechut* is not that of a facilitator of Torah but equal to Torah itself (see *Sotah* 21a; also below pp. 93-94). To our wonderful children—Malkah Rachel, Matisyahu Nachum (Hagit), Deena (Adam), and Yehudah Zevi, as well as to our grandchildren, Ellin, Netalya, and Alexandra—a *Birchat Kohan BeAhavah* for the blessings of Torah to sanctify their lives.

Special tribute and appreciation must be extended to the mentors of our family—unique parents who serve as our models for Torah and *chesed:* My father, HaRav HaGaon Reb Meir Cohen (*zecher tzaddik livrachah*) former *menahel* of the Agudat HaRabonim and author of *Chelkat Meir*, volumes I and II; my mother, Rebbetzen Itka Cohen (*tichyeh*); my father-in-law, HaRav HaGaon Reb Yaakov Nayman, Shlita, the noted Brisker Talmid Chacham and Rav of Congregation Adat B'nai Yisrael, Chicago, Illinois; my mother-in-law, Rebbetzen Chaya Nayman *(tichyeh)*. It is they who have infused our lives with meaning and joy. It is their love of Torah that has graced our lives.

A special *Todah LaHashem* for the *zechut* of serving as Rav of Congregation Shaarei Tefila; a synagogue noted for Torah leadership, philanthropy, and communal concern.

The first edition of this book was originally published over ten years ago. At that time, I gave a copy to the Chief Rabbi of Israel, HaRav HaGaon Rabbi Avraham Kahana Shapiro. Noting it contained Halachic discourses, he asked me whether it was my first book. When I responded affirmatively, he related the following: "The great rabbinic sage, HaRav HaGaon R. Meir Simcha of D'vinsk, at a young age wrote two books. One was an interpretation of Biblical verses; the other, a Halachic analysis of the laws of the Rambam. R. Meir Simcha wanted to first publish his Bible commentary for he felt that it most succinctly expressed his views. He was advised otherwise, for should he first publish such a work, he would be known as a preacher rather than a Talmudic scholar. So too," concluded the Chief Rabbi, "this applies to you. Now that you established expertise in Talmud with this volume, you can write about other matters." My problem is that the more I study Talmud and Halachah, the more I recognize how little I know and how much more it is necessary to study. There is simply no time to devote to other matters.

Dedication to the Lubavitcher Rebbe, *Shlita*

In an effort to unify Jewish youth, the Lubavitcher Rebbe, *Shlita*, initiated a sacred worldwide mission of writing *Sifrei Torah* expressly for children. Each child was granted an enviable, rare opportunity of having a holy letter in a *Sefer Torah* expressly consecrated and written in his (or her) behalf. This endeavor generated a unique positive appreciation for the *mitzvah* of writing a *Sefer Torah* and served simultaneously as a prime catalyst for its popularization. It is difficult to conceive of an era in which more Jews were so actively involved with this *mitzvah*. The purpose of the Rebbe was to symbolize the *achdut* (unity) of our Jewish children.

What is unique, apart from any symbolic goal of unity, is that this effort appears to be the first time in modern history that Jewish children have received practical education in the *mitzvah* of writing a *Sefer Torah*. Adults are mandated to *m'chanech* (educate) children in the performance of *mitzvot*. Prior to Bar Mitzvah we are even *m'chanech* children in the *mitzvah* of *tefillin*. Why, then, are we not *m'chanech* children in the *mitzvah* of writing a *Sefer Torah*?

Indeed, this was not always the case. The Talmud states that an *apotropos* was mandated to acquire for minor orphan children in his care a *Sefer Torah* as well as *tefillin* and *Mezuzot* (*Gittin* 52a). The Rambam says that he was to acquire these for orphans even though, as minors, they were not obligated in any of the *mitzvot* except through the purpose of *chinnuch* (Rambam, *Laws of Nachalot*, chap. 11, law 10).

In other words, the *apotropos*, who is basically an executor for an orphan minor child, must acquire a *Sefer Torah* for the child even though the child is a minor and as such is only involved in the *mitzvah* because of *chinnuch* (education). Thus, there is precedent for the process of *chinnuch* in the *mitzvah* of writing a *Sefer Torah*.

The Halachah states that if an *apotropos* commences efforts in behalf of an orphan, he cannot relinquish his obligations. He cannot decide that he no longer wishes to serve in behalf of the child. Why is this so? Doesn't any employee have the right to decide that he no longer wishes to work? The distinction is as follows. All employees are servants of God, not man. Thus, no one may be coerced to work against his will. As a free, independent soul, one may, at any time decide that he no longer wishes to work for a specific person. An *apotropos*, however, is not simply an employee or trustee of an estate. He is not performing a professional function but a *mitzvah*, a religious obligation, and one cannot relinquish the continual performance of such a holy task (*Kezot HaChoshen, Choshen Mishpat* 290).

The unique *mitzvah* of *chinnuch* crystallized by the Rebbe suggests that the Rebbe serves in the role of *apotropos* for our Jewish children, who in our day are *yetomim bechayyei aveihem*. They are religious orphans who require a spiritual father. Once their *apotropos* has commenced his efforts, he must continue.

Anything done in the world can be equaled or excelled by another except the quality of being first. No one can equal that role. By attempting to create unity, the Rebbe has simultaneously established the posture of being first in developing *chinnuch* for the *mitzvah* of writing a *Sefer Torah*.

As a result of the Rebbe's intense involvement with this *mitzvah*, numerous individuals have begun to learn and relearn the *mitzvah* of writing a *Sefer Torah*. The *Chiddushei Torah* in this volume are, therefore, dedicated to the Rebbe in recognition of his unique stature as the modern-day spiritual father of this *mitzvah*.

1

The *Mitzvah* to Write a *Sefer Torah*: Basic Concepts

AN ANALYSIS OF THE MITZVAH

Tradition has it that there are 613 primary Biblical commandments, of which the 613th is the *mitzvah* of writing a *Sefer Torah* (see *Sefer HaChinnuch*). In articulating the dimensions of this *mitzvah*, the Rambam (Maimonides) notes that "it is a positive Biblical command for *every single Jewish male* to write a *Sefer Torah* for himself" (Free translation—Rambam, *Laws of Tefillin, Mezuzah, and Sefer Torah*, chap. 7, law 1).

Since the Rambam is quite precise in his use of terminology, special attention should be paid to any instance of apparently excess wordage. The phrase stipulating that "every single Jewish male" is obligated to write a *Sefer Torah* appears somewhat redundant. Could not the Rambam have merely stated that the *mitzvah* was incumbent upon "every Jewish male"?

It is suggested that the Rambam is endeavoring to emphasize the personal nature of the *mitzvah*. By specifying that the obligation is upon "every single Jewish male," he is forestalling any possible confusion of the *mitzvah* to write a *Sefer Torah* with the general *mitzvah* of acquiring a *Sefer Torah* for communal synagogal use. Indeed, Jews who reside in a community are required to establish a synagogue and acquire a *Sefer Torah* for public Torah reading (Rambam, *Laws of Prayer*, chap. 11, law 1). Thus, by careful utilization of emphasis, the Rambam is stating that the *mitzvah* of writing a *Sefer Torah* is incumbent upon each and every Jew apart from any communal obligation. This means that even if one resides in a community which has more than enough *Sifrei Torah* to meet its synagogal obligations, each Jew is still mandated to either write himself or commission a scribe to write by hand a copy of the Pentateuch on parchment in order to comply with his personal *mitzvah* of writing a *Sefer Torah*.

In light of this, the common practice of commissioning a scribe to write a *Sefer Torah* and subsequently donating the Torah to the community appears to be incongruous to the nature of the *mitzvah*. If the Biblical *mitzvah* does not have a communal aspect, logic would presume that the *Sefer Torah* should not be donated to a synagogue but, rather, retained as the personal, private possession of the owner.

Indeed, some rabbinic authorities contend that the *mitzvah* is not only to write a *Sefer Torah* but to retain possession of it. This view is based upon the Halachic assumption that if someone loses his *Sefer Torah*, he is required to write another in order to fulfill the mandate of the *mitzvah*. Thus, the donation of a *Sefer Torah* to a synagogue, according to this view, is basically a negation of the *mitzvah*, for a communal *Sefer Torah* belongs to all and by definition eliminates any exclusivity of personal ownership. It is in the same category as having lost a *Sefer Torah* (see *Torat Chayyim, Sanhedrin* 21b; also Codes, *Shulchan Aruch Yoreh De'ah* 270, Glosses of Rav Akiva Eiger, ibid., *Pitchai Teshuvah*, note 3).

Accordingly, donating a Torah to a synagogue would impose upon the donor an obligation to write another *Sefer Torah* to fulfill the personal Biblical *mitzvah*. Another suggested solution is that the donor restrict the terms of the public grant, permitting the community merely to house the *Sefer Torah* and read from it but not to sell it, since ownership is retained by the donor (Rambam, *Laws of Sefer Torah*, Chap. 7, see *Sefer Kovetz*).

The aforementioned orientation somewhat diminishes the luster of the festivity associated with donating a *Sefer Torah* to a synagogue. It implies that the donation to the community has no relationship to the original *mitzvah* of writing a *Sefer Torah*. It even calls into question the necessity of such a donation when the synagogue already has numerous *Sifrei Torah* available for use. However, since common practice throughout the world since medieval times has both sanctified and extolled this custom, it is apparent that different guidelines and nuances of meaning are operative.

Rabbenu Asher (Rosh) articulated a novel theory concerning the nature of the *mitzvah* of writing a *Sefer Torah*. He contended that the prime purpose was to study Torah from the *Sefer Torah* itself. In other words, each Jew was required to possess a *Sefer Torah* in order to facilitate Torah learning. In early times, this was, indeed, the practice. To the extent that the custom changed—for people no longer utilized the *Sefer Torah* as a text for Torah learning but placed it in a synagogue for use in public Torah readings—Rabbenu Asher noted that one may fulfill the mitzvah by acquiring texts of Bible, Mishnah, Talmud, and commentaries. The *Beit Yosef* (the author of the codes of the *Shulchan Aruch*) clarified this position by firmly stating that Rabbenu Asher was in no way suggesting that the *Mitzvah* to write *Sefer Torah* had been eliminated in modern times. Indeed, Rabbenu Asher was not even maintaining that the acquisition of Bible texts was on a par with writing a *Sefer Torah*. Rabbenu Asher was merely establishing the principle that religious texts should also be obtained in order to fulfill the purpose of the *mitzvah*, which is the study of Torah (see *Tur Shulchan Aruch, Yoreh De'ah* 270; also *Beit Yosef* and *Bach*).

This viewpoint that the study of Torah is the prime purpose of the *Mitzvah* of writing a *Sefer Torah* appears to be corroborated by Scripture, for the Biblical command to write a *Sefer Torah* is followed by the phrase "and teach it to the children of Israel" (Deuteronomy 31:19). Indeed, when Moses complied with the command to write a *Sefer Torah*, the Bible notes that he "taught it to the children of Israel" (Deuteronomy 31:22). (Note also the first use of the term *Sefer Hatorah*, Deuteronomy 31:26.)

The difficulty with this theory is that the Talmud states that the acquisition of a *Sefer Torah* through inheritance does not fulfill the mandate of the *mitzvah*. A son who inherits a *Sefer*

Torah is obligated to write another *Sefer Torah* to fulfill his own personal *mitzvah* (see *Sanhedrin* 21b; also Rambam, *Laws of Sefer Torah*, chap. 7, law 1). If, however, the purpose of writing a *Sefer Torah* is to learn Torah, what difference does it make whether he learns with his father's or his own *Sefer Torah?* The knowledge learned is the same. On the basis of this question, some authorities have rejected Torah learning as the purpose of the *mitzvah* (see Shagat Aryeh 36).

Some contend, however, that this question does not negate Rabbenu Asher's theory but, rather, enhances its meaning. For example, on Sukkot one is permitted to fulfill the personal *mitzvah* of *etrog* with an *etrog* acquired through inheritance, but one is not permitted to observe the *mitzvah* of writing a *Sefer Torah* with a Torah obtained in the same way. Why is this so? On Sukkot, the *mitzvah* is to have an *etrog* and make a blessing over it. There is no interest in increasing the amount of *etrogim* in the world. The *mitzvah* of writing a *Sefer Torah*, however, is for the purpose of providing a text that can be utilized for study. An increase in the number of *Sifrei Torah* definitely facilitates an increase in Torah study, for as more *Sifrei Torah* become available, more individuals are able to study. Indeed, the Talmud states that R. Ammi, who was wealthy, wrote four hundred *Sifrei Torah* (*Bava Batra* 14a). Obviously, the purpose was to make more texts available for students, and thus increase the amount of Torah studied. If a person were able to observe the mitzvah of writing a *Sefer Torah* by obtaining one through inheritance, Torah study would be inhibited. Each father would bequeath his Torah to his son. After several generations the number of *Sifrei* Torah available for Torah study would be diminished. This, in turn, would limit the number of students having access to Torah texts. Therefore, in order to safeguard the proliferation of *Sifrei Torah* in the world, the Halachah prohibits observing the *mitzvah* with a Torah acquired through inheritance. (A restrictive aspect of this reasoning would be the negation of the observance of the *mitzvah* by buying a *Sefer Torah* from a previous owner, for observing the *mitzvah* by purchase would also serve to limit the process of increasing *Sifrei Torah* throughout the Jewish community and thus would be comparable to inheritance [See R. Baruch Epstein, *Tosefet Berachah*, Deuteronomy, *Parashat Vayelech*, pp. 241–242].) See also *Sefer HaChinnuch* (*mitzvah* 613), who rules that every Jew must have a personal *Sefer Torah* so that one who wishes to learn Torah need not go to another's house for study. Also, an inherited *Sefer Torah* is disallowed for purposes of the *mitzvah* in order to increase the number of *Sifrei Torah* available.

DONATING A SEFER TORAH TO A SYNAGOGUE

The line of thought developed in the preceding section may also serve as the rationale for the custom of donating a *Sefer Torah* to a synagogue. If an integral aspect of the *mitzvah* is to increase the use of the *Sefer Torah*, then by granting the *Sefer Torah* to a community the donor is facilitating such expanded service. The Torah is no longer the exclusive possession of the owner. Others, a whole community, now have access to the text. Indeed, the act of conveying the Torah to the synagogue serves as a prominent manifestation of the fulfillment of the highest purpose of the *mitzvah*.

Even in ancient times, when the *Sefer Torah* was utilized as a basic text for study, the custom of donating it to a synagogue may have been extolled. The housing of a *Sefer Torah* in a synagogue facilitated increased access by numerous students for purposes of study. Even when *Sifrei Torah* were no longer used as texts, the custom persisted, for a communal *Sefer Torah* had a greater usage than a personal one.

As a result, someone who donated a *Sefer Torah* to a synagogue would *not* be obligated to write another *Sefer Torah* to fulfill his personal *Mitzvah*. Indeed, there would be also no reason to restrict the terms of the grant to the synagogue. Yet if the donor, for personal reasons, decided that he wished to maintain ultimate possession of the *Sefer Torah*, he would still be complying with the purpose of the *mitzvah* as long as the community had full access and usage. Indeed, there does not appear to be any valid basis for the Halachic assumption that a

Sefer Torah lost or removed from exclusive possession obligates the writing of another one.

It is known that a *Sefer Torah* generally should not be sold. Under dire circumstances, however, it may be sold for the purpose of learning Torah or for marriage (see Rambam, *Laws of Sefer Torah*, chap. 10, law 2). If the sale of a *Sefer Torah* negates the fulfillment of the *mitzvah*, why is there no mention of the seller eliminating his previous *mitzvah* and being mandated to write another *Sefer Torah*? The conclusion is obvious. Subsequent removal of ownership does not in any way detract from the *mitzvah* of writing a *Sefer Torah*.

There is one Halachah which may suggest a possible basis for the assumption that continued possession of the *Sefer Torah* is an integral part of the *mitzvah*. Apart from the *Sefer Torah* that every Jew is required to write, a king was obligated to write a second *Sefer Torah* (see Deuteronomy 17:18). In rulings relating to the king's *Sifrei Torah*, the Rambam notes that if a king lost a *Sefer Torah* he was required to write another (Rambam, *Laws of Kings*, chap. 3, law 1). The implication is that loss of possession invalidates the *mitzvah*. Just as this law is applicable to the *Sifrei Torah* required of a king, so too should it refer to the *Sefer Torah* mandated upon all Jews.

It may be demonstrated, however, that no general principle may be derived from this specific ruling. First of all, if loss of possession invalidates the *mitzvah*, then the Rambam should have said so in his general discussion of the laws of a *Sefer Torah*. Why was this ruling only stated in a listing of laws pertaining to a king's *Sefer Torah*? The logical assumption is that the ruling requiring continued possession relates only to the king's *Sefer Torah* and not to the *Sefer Torah* required of all Jews. In other words, there is an aspect of the nature of the king's *Sefer Torah* that requires continued possession. The Rambam, in fact, clearly delineates the uses of the king's two *Sifrei Torah*. One, of course, was the *Sefer Torah* required of all Jews. The king, despite his exalted position, shared the common Jew's obligation to write a *Sefer Torah*. This *Sefer Torah*, the Rambam states, was "placed in his treasury house." The second *Sefer*

Torah, the one the king had to write in his role as king, "had to be with him permanently." "Should he go to war, the *Sefer Torah* was with him; . . . when he entered an assemblage, sat in judgment, . . . the Torah was with him. As it is written, 'and it shall be with him, and he shall read therein all the days of his life' [Deuteronomy 17:19]" (see Rambam, *Laws of Sefer Torah*, chap. 7, laws 2, 3; also Rambam, *Laws of Kings*, chap. 3, law 1). Thus, the *Sefer Torah* required of a king had a specific and ongoing purpose. It was an appendage to the king—a constant symbol of his royal title. He was normally required to have it with him at all times. Moreover, he could not utilize the *Sefer Torah* written for his father when his father was king—each king had to write his own *Sefer Torah* to symbolize his assumption of reign. As a result, the king's special *Sefer Torah* could not be lost—it had to be available for use at all times. Should it be lost, however, then, of course, the king would be obligated to write another *Sefer Torah* to meet his royal requirement to constantly manifest its presence. The *Sefer Torah* required of all Jews, however, had no such stipulation of constant usage. Thus, there is no basis for the assumption that losing a *Sefer Torah* invalidates the *mitzvah*. (Even if one presumed that the loss of a *Sefer Torah* was a problem, since logically such a situation would imply a possible lack of utilization, the donation of a *Sefer Torah* to a synagogue would mitigate this factor.)

What is still somewhat problematic is the description of the use of the king's other *Sefer Torah*, the one required of him as a Jew like other Jews. As previously noted, the Rambam states that this *Sefer Torah* was to be placed in the king's treasury house—in other words, it was placed in storage. The Rambam only describes the king's requirement to utilize the special *Sefer Torah* written expressly as a symbol of his kingship. Yet if the *Sefer Torah* required of all Jews was for the purpose of learning Torah or, at least, of facilitating use of the Torah, why is no mention made of any need to utilize it? In other words, once this *Sefer Torah* was written, no further involvement was mandated. Why? The Biblical command for the king to write a special *Sefer Torah* does not eliminate the requirement for the king to write a *Sefer Torah* like all other Jews; similarly, the *mitzvah* of constantly learning and showing the king's *Sefer Torah* should not diminish the need to use the other *Sefer Torah*. However, the Rambam makes no reference to any purpose served by the general *Sefer Torah*, implying that Torah study is not the prime motivation for the *mitzvah*. Thus the Rambam's position would definitely seem to be that the *mitzvah* is completed upon the culmination of the scribal function. If so, then what is the *raison d'être* for writing a *Sefer Torah*?

An approach to the meaning of the *mitzvah* can be gleaned from an understanding of the Talmudic citation that describes certain people as "fools, for they rise before a *Sefer Torah*, and not before a great scholar" (who presumably has mastered the Torah) (see *Makkot* 22b). This statement is difficult to comprehend. Since the custom is labeled as "foolish," the implication is that the so-called foolishness is readily noticeable. Yet this is not the case. The *Sefer Torah* is accorded by Halachah the highest degree of *Kedushah* ("holy sanctity") of all the ritual objects used in the performance of *mitzvot*. No other ritual object in any way compares to the *Sefer Torah*. As a result, it is certainly understandable why these people singled out the *Sefer Torah* for unique deference.

R. Shlomo Kluger suggests that the laws relating to the proper method of writing a *Sefer Torah* make it possible to understand this Talmudic citation as well as the nature of the *mitzvah* itself. What creates, he asks, the sanctity of a *Sefer Torah*? Is it not the quality of the person who wrote it? Without the input of a human scribe, Hebrew letters on parchment do not establish a status of *kedushah* for a scroll. Indeed, even a scroll written by hand by a scribe is not deemed as holy unless proper intentions of sanctity permeated the entire process. Thus, it is within the power of a human being to crystallize the *kedushah* of a *Sefer Torah*. Now if a human can establish the holiness of a parchment scroll, surely he can create a posture of *kedushah* for himself. This shows the foolishness of the custom cited above. The "fools" mentioned in the Talmud recognize the power of man to sanctify a scroll of parchment, and thus afford the scroll great deference, but do not comprehend the ability of man to transform himself into a vehicle of sanctity by mastering the Torah. What man can give to a piece of parchment he certainly can establish for himself. This, concludes R. Shlomo Kluger, is the motivation for the *mitzvah* of writing a *Sefer Torah*: the obligation of each Jew to appreciate man's potential potency—to recognize that it is in man's power to create *kedushah*, and that the *mitzvah* of writing a *Sefer Torah* implants respect for the holiness of rabbinic scholars and Torah. The *kedushah* of a *Sefer Torah* demonstrates the *kedushah* of Torah knowledge (see basic concept, *Responsa Tuv Ta'am VeDa'at*, part 1, responsum 231).

This theory, although not generally known, certainly sheds light upon the entire *mitzvah* and its various laws. Now it is possible to understand why a Jew may not observe the *mitzvah* by utilizing a *Sefer Torah* acquired through inheritance. Every Jew must himself perceive the ability of Torah scholars to create *kedushah*. This sacred sense of appreciation is an obligation that must be personally assumed. The fact that one's father manifested this recognition is not automatically transferable to the son. In addition, there is now a clear line of demarcation between the two *Sifrei Torah* required of the king. One *Sefer Torah* was to foster an intense appreciation of the potential power of Torah scholars to create holiness. Once it was written, it had no practical use and could, therefore, be stored in the king's treasure house. The second *Sefer Torah*, the one required only of kings, was needed for regular study and had to be constantly with the king. This theory may also explain the reason for the interrelationship of the *mitzvah* of writing a *Sefer Torah* and the practice of donating a *Sefer Torah* to a synagogue. If the purpose of the *mitzvah* is to manifest an appreciation of *kedushah*, then the logical extension of this *mitzvah* is to donate the *Sefer Torah* to a synagogue. After all, what makes a synagogue holy? Is it not hallowed by the prayers of Jews? Is it not a place of sacred devotion sanctified by the performance of community prayers? Even without a *Sefer Torah*, a permanent house of worship has a degree of *kedushah*. It is a place whose walls exude a hallowness of sanctity, for the past, present, and future needs of Jews echo within its chambers. Jewish prayer made it holy. Jews unified in supplication to the Almighty created the *kedushah*. Since a *Sefer Torah* becomes a vehicle of kedushah, and thus is a treasure in itself, the king could not store it in any mundane area—it had to be kept with his most prized possessions, with his treasures. Where was the common Jew to store his treasured *Sefer Torah*? Was not the synagogue the most logical place? A *Sefer Torah*, which teaches the power of but one man to create *kedushah*, certainly should be kept in the place that signifies the power of a community to create *kedushah*. By donating a *Sefer Torah* to a synagogue, the owner is relating the power of one man to the potency of a community to establish *kedushah*. This is yet another recognition of the heights Jews may attain. It is a further, deeper, and more sensitive extension of the belief that holiness is in the hands of the Jewish people.

For this reason, festivities are celebrated when a *Sefer Torah* is donated. When Jews manifest appreciation of the role of *Kedushah*—this is the height of Jewish joy.

2

The Original *Sefer Torah* and *Keri'at Hatorah*

THE MIDRASH THAT MOSHE RABBENU WROTE THIRTEEN SIFREI TORAH

According to the Midrash, Moshe Rabbenu wrote thirteen *Sifrei Torah* on the day of his death. One of them was given to each of the twelve tribes, and the thirteenth was placed in the Ark (*aron*) of the Sanctuary, so that it could be brought out (to validate the issue) if an attempt were ever made to falsify the Torah (*Midrash Rabbah*, Deuteronomy, *Parashah 9, Vayelech*).

Rabbenu Asher quotes this Midrash to refute the claim that Moshe Rabbenu died on Shabbat. A position had been articulated that Torah should not be publicly studied on Shabbat between the *Minchah*, and *Ma'ariv* services, the rationale being that since Moshe Rabbenu had died (supposedly) during that time, formal Torah study should cease as a form of public memorial. Rabbenu Asher notes that Moshe Rabbenu could not have died on Shabbat, for if he had, how could he have written the *Sifrei Torah*, thus violating the Shabbat? He concludes that Moshe Rabbenu passed away on a Friday (Rabbenu Asher, *Pesachim*, chap. 10, no. 13).

From this Midrash and Rabbenu Asher's commentary proceed a variety of interesting observations. R. Aaron Levin (Rav of Raysha) comments on the sheer impossibility of one man writing so many *Sifrei Torah* in one day. He suggests, therefore, that Moshe Rabbenu wrote the *Sifrei Torah* prior to the seventh

17

of Adar (the traditional *Yahrzeit* of Moshe Rabbenu) and on the
day of his demise merely concluded the process. Just as there is
a general rule that the status of a *mitzvah* is granted only upon
the completion of an act *(Sotah 13b)*, so too in terms of time—
that is, the date when the *mitzvah* was completed is the decisive
element in regard to time, and not the date when the process
began *(Responsa Avnei Chayfetz 80, part 9)*.

A somewhat different solution to the problem may be presented. It is known that Moshe Rabbenu wrote at least one *Sefer
Torah*, for Scripture states that he wrote a Torah and gave it to
the *kohanim* and the elders (Deuteronomy 31:9). Rashi notes
that when he completed the Torah he gave it to his tribe (ibid).
Subsequently, Scripture notes that when Moshe Rabbenu concluded the Torah, he directed that it be placed adjacent to the
holy tablets (see Deuteronomy, 31:24–26). Ramban suggests
that this was the same *Sefer Torah* previously given to the
kohanim, but that Moshe Rabbenu did not stipulate where it
should be located until it was concluded (Deuteronomy 31:24).
The following points should be noted:

1. It is possible to conjecture that Moshe Rabbenu only wrote
   one *Sefer Torah*. The additional twelve *Sifrei Torah* were
   written but not completed by others, who utilized Moshe's
   Torah as the authoritative text. On the day of his death,
   Moshe Rabbenu completed all thirteen *Sifrei Torah*. This may
   be the source of the Talmudic citation that "if one corrects
   even one letter it is considered as if he wrote [an entire *Sefer
   Torah*]" *(Menachot 30a)*.

2. If the Halachah is that continual possession of a *Sefer Torah* is
   an integral aspect of the *mitzvah* of writing a *Sefer Torah*, why
   did Moshe Rabbenu not write fourteen rather than thirteen
   Sifrei Torah, retaining one as a means of performing his own
   mitzvah? Since it is evident that Moshe Rabbenu did not
   retain a *Sefer Torah* for himself, it certainly would seem that
   possession and/or ownership of a *Sefer Torah* is not relevant
   to the *mitzvah* at all.

3. Why did Moshe Rabbenu give a *Sefer Torah* to each tribe?
   And why did he make a point of doing so on the day of his

death? It is suggested that this Midrash is the key to the understanding of a Talmudic citation relating to the establishment of *Keri'at Hatorah*.

THE RELATIONSHIP OF THE MITZVAH TO KERI'AT HATORAH

The Talmud *(Bava Kamma* 82a) notes that Ezra ordained that the Torah should be read (publicly) in the *Minchah* service on Shabbat as well as on Mondays and Thursdays. Concerning the latter two periods of time, the Talmud states that (public) Torah readings were enacted even prior to Ezra. "For the early prophets enacted that the Torah should be read on Shabbat . . . Mondays . . . and Thursdays, so that they [*Kelal Yisrael*] should not be three days without Torah." Thus, Ezra's ordinances were apparently superfluous. To this the Talmud responds that the original decree was that "one man should read three verses or that three men should together read three verses, corresponding to *kohanim, levi'im,* and *yisraelim*. Ezra then came and ordained that three men should be called up to read (in the Torah) and that ten verses should be read."

From this citation it is evident that all agree that the early prophets were the only ones who established *Keri'at HaTorah* on Shabbat, for the discussion relates only to Mondays and Thursdays. Yet the motivation for the establishment of *keri'at HaTorah* on Shabbat is not clear. The Talmud contends that *Keri'at HaTorah* on Mondays and Thursdays was ordained so that three days should not pass without Torah. Utilizing Shabbat as the base coupled with the three-day requirement, it is understandable why Mondays and Thursdays required *Keri'at HaTorah*. Yet no explanation is presented as to why Shabbat was selected as the base unit of time.

Rambam ruled that it was Moshe Rabbenu himself who enacted the ordinance that there should be public readings of the Torah on Shabbat *(Hilchot Tefillah,* chap. 12, law 1). Commenting upon this apparent deviation from the Talmud, which cites the early prophets as the originators of this ordinance, the

Kesef Mishneh clarifies the issue by noting that the Rambam is not disputing the Talmudic citation. The Rambam is, rather, of the opinion that since Moshe Rabbenu was the greatest prophet in that era, the decree of *Keri'at HaTorah* was promulgated either through his *bet din* or with his acquiescence (ibid).

According to Rabbenu Asher, Moshe Rabbenu died on a Friday and concluded the *Sifrei Torah* on that day. Since Shabbat would thus appear to have been the first opportunity available to conduct a public reading of the Torah, Moshe Rabbenu presented each tribe with a *Sefer Torah* on the day of his death, Friday, so that all of them could observe the decree of *Keri'at HaTorah* the next day, Shabbat. Each tribe, as a self-contained community, received a *Sefer Torah* of its own.

Thus, the act of writing a *Sefer Torah* and granting it to a synagogue may be a way of emulating the role of the first writer of a *Sefer Torah*, Moshe Rabbenu. Moreover, the *Keri'at HaTorah* may be more closely intertwined with the *mitzvah* of writing a *Sefer Torah* than is generally noted. Indeed, the *Keri'at HaTorah* may have been instituted as a continuing testament to Moshe Rabbenu's life, a means of ensuring public knowledge of Torah for future generations after his death.

THE COMMUNAL ROLE OF *KERI'AT* HATORAH

The very fact that each tribe had thousands of men, and that such vast numbers precluded all from actually hearing the Torah when it was read publicly, does not pose an Halachic challenge to the above-noted theory. Even though some Halachic authorities contend that it is an obligation to hear every word of the *Keri'at HaTorah* (see *Mishnah Berurah, Orach Chayyim, Hilchot Shabbat* 285:14, who notes the concurrence of the *Magen Avraham* and the Vilna Gaon), the final Halachah is not clear on this matter. Indeed, it appears probable that the *mitzvah* was a communal obligation and not necessarily a mandate upon every single Jew. In other words, every community has an obligation to read the Torah in the presense of at least ten Jews. No one may walk out, disturb others, or act indifferent to the *Keri'at HaTorah*, for such are acts of disrespect (see *Berachot* 8a). It is even probable that while in the synagogue one must be attentive to each word read to ensure that at least a *minyan* hears the *Keri'at HaTorah*. Yet should an individual miss part of the *Keri'at HaTorah* (or even all of it), there is no Halachic requirement to take out the Torah and read it again to enable him to fulfill his personal obligation.

Tosafot (*Sukkah* 52a) reports that the synagogue in Alexandria was so large that when a person had an *aliyah* to the Torah, a flag would be waved to signal the conclusion of the *berachah* so that the congregation could respond by chanting Amen. Now, if the congregation could not hear the *berachot*, it is obvious that they also could not hear the *Keri'at HaTorah*. Yet the synagogue conducted public readings of the Torah knowing full well that all could not hear the proceedings. The logical answer is that as long as a quorum of ten Jews heard the *Keri'at HaTorah*, it was sufficient to meet the requirement. Those who did not hear the *Keri'at HaTorah* were not obligated to reread the Torah. As long as they worshipped in a synagogue where the Torah was publicly read (even if they did not hear it), they were absolved from all personal requirements.

On Purim there is a requirement to read the *Megillah* even without a *minyan* (*Shulchan Aruch, Orach Chayyim* 690:18, glosses of Rama). There is no such stipulation for *Keri'at HaTorah* throughout the year.

R. Yaakov of Lissa (*Chavvat Da'at*) ruled that those who quietly learn Torah by themselves while the *Sefer Torah* is being read should not be rebuked, for they have Halachic authorities to rely upon (*yesh lahem ma-lesmach*) (*Derech HaChayyim, Laws of Communal Behavior during Keri'at HaTorah*, law 4). Yet he notes that such behavior is not permissible during the reading of *Parashot Zachor* and *Parah* (ibid., law 6). The distinction is clear. *Keri'at HaTorah* is a communal ordinance, but the others are personal obligations.

The *Aruch HaShulchan* (*Hilchot Keri'at HaTorah* 146:5) restricts independent Torah study during *Keri'at HaTorah* to advanced professional scholars but concludes, on the basis of the practical consideration that such activities might induce a disrespect for *Keri'at HaTorah* among ordinary laymen, that it should be prohibited. In other words, one must be attentive to the *Keri'at HaTorah* for secondary reasons.

R. Henkin, the previous *posek hador* and righteous director of Ezras Torah, explicitly stated that "the reading of the *Megillah* is a more stringent requirement than *Keri'at HaTorah*, for the former is an obligation upon each and every person, while the latter is only a communal requirement. Thus, should a person miss even one word of the *Megillah*, he is required to reread the entire *Megillah*." *(Edut LeYisrael,* p. 134). There is no such mandate for *Keri'at HaTorah*.

Thus, even though the majority of the Jews in the wilderness may not have heard the *Keri'at HaTorah*, this would not have invalidated the process.

KERI'AT HATORAH FOR SHABBAT

The Jerusalem Talmud states that Moshe ordained *Keri'at HaTorah* for Shabbat, Yom Tov, Chol HaMo'ed, and Rosh Chodesh, as is written, "And Moshe ordained the appointed seasons of the Lord [*mo'adei HaShem*] to the Children of Israel" (Leviticus 23:44; Yerushalmi, *Megillah* 29a; see also Rif, *Megillah*, chap. 4). The *Bach* cites this Yerushalmi to sustain the view that *Keri'at HaTorah* is a Biblical *mitzvah*, and that Ezra's function was to establish the order of the *parshiyot (Tur, Shulchan Aruch, Orach Chayyim* 685; see also Taz, ibid.).

The *Magen Avraham* appears to disregard the Scriptural basis for *Keri'at HaTorah* and suggests that just as Ezra's role related only to the number of *aliyot* on Monday and Thursday, so Moshe's function pertained only to the number of *aliyot* for Shabbat, Yom Tov, etc. *(Schulchan Aruch, Orach Chayyim* 135:1).

The *Peri Megadim* notes that the consensus of Halachic authorities is that *Keri'at HaTorah* is not a Biblical *mitzvah* but, rather, an ancient tradition classified as *divrei kabbalah*. The above-cited Biblical verse, moreover, is merely a Rabbinic reference to Scripture called an *asmakhta (Mishbatzot Zahav, Orach Chayyim* 135 and 685).

Yet, since *Keri'at HaTorah* is deemed *divrei kabbalah*, it manifests a higher degree of sanctity than a mere Rabbinic ordinance. As a result, since minors are mandated to observe *Keri'at HaTorah* because of the Rabbinic *mitzvah* of *Chinnuch*, a minor cannot serve as a *ba'al koreh* for a legal adult, whose obligation is derived from *divrei Kabbalah*. Also, in matters of *safek* (doubt), cases of *divrei kabbalah* are decided on a stringent basis (like a Biblical law) rather than on a lenient consideration (like a Rabbinic rule) (*Peri Megadim, Orach Chayyim, Igeret* 2, General Introduction, Rule 18; see *Magen Avraham, Orach Chayyim* 282).

The Babylonian Talmud, citing the verse, "And Moshe ordained the *mo'adei HaShem* to the Children of Israel," comments "that it is a *mitzvah* that each should be read in its proper time" (Mishnah, *Megillah* 31a). Rashi notes that the verse teaches us that "it is a *mitzvah* to read on a *mo'ed* something pertaining to the *mo'ed* itself." Thus, on each Yom Tov we read a portion of the Torah which relates to some matter applicable to the Yom Tov. Yet on Shabbat the *Keri'at HaTorah* does not relate at all to Shabbat. This implies that the Babylonian Talmud does not include Shabbat in the Scriptural mandate for *Keri'at HaTorah*. Why? Though Shabbat is included in the general category of *mo'adim* (see Leviticus 23:1–3), the Torah does not mention Shabbat when it stipulates that "these are the *mo'adei HaShem* . . . which you shall proclaim in its season [*bemo'ado*]" (v. 4). This suggests that the *mitzvah* to read the Torah is limited to those *mo'adim* which require reference to the *mo'ed* on the day of the *mo'ed* itself (see Maharsha, *Megillah* 32, who suggests that the *mitzvah* of *Keri'at HaTorah* is based on Leviticus 23:4).

The *Netziv* provides a rationale as to why the normal reading of the Torah is suspended on Yom Tov and only portions related to the Yom Tov are read. He contends that *Keri'at HaTorah* for Yom Tov is derived from Scripture, while *Keri'at HaTorah* for Shabbat is an ordinance of Moshe. Since the Torah readings for Yom Tov are, therefore, on a higher level of sanctity than the readings for Shabbat, it would not be correct to preface the regular Shabbat *Keri'at HaTorah* prior to that of Yom Tov. Also, to read the Yom Tov portion before the regular *parashah* would not be feasible, for the *Keri'at HaTorah* for Shabbat is more frequent (*tadir*) than the Yom Tov readings, and there is a general rule that in matters of priority, the more frequent case takes precedence. As a result, the regular readings for Shabbat were eliminated (Rav Naftali Tzevi Hirsch Berlin, *Meromei Sadeh, Megillah* 30b).

The *Tzemach Tzedek* discusses various Halachic ramifications of a minor serving as a *ba'al koreh*. His conclusion is that a minor may serve as a *ba'al koreh* only on Shabbat afternoon, for such readings were ordained by Ezra (Commentary *Megillah*, chap. 3). The implication is that at other times the mandate for *Keri'at HaTorah* has a greater degree of sanctity and importance, and minors cannot represent adults.

The *Meiri*, in his classic treatise on the Laws of a *Sefer Torah* entitled *Kiryat Sefer*, notes that a minor may have an *aliyah* subsequent to the *aliyah* of an adult, for in such circumstances the *Keri'at HaTorah* enacted by Moshe Rabbenu is concluded and the subsequent readings come under the category of Ezra's ordinance (*Ma'amar* 5, Part 1). Thus, even on Shabbat morning *Keri'at HaTorah* contains a combination of both Moshe's and Ezra's ordinances. If so, then once three verses are read or three people have an *aliyah* (see *Bava Kamma* 82a), a minor would be able to serve as *ba'al koreh*.

(The *Meiri*, moreover, notes [ibid.] that since others are required to teach Torah to a minor, he is, therefore, involved in Talmud Torah and may properly recite the *Birchat HaTorah*.)

It may be demonstrated that *Keri'at HaTorah* for Shabbat underwent several structural changes.

> R. Yochanan said that one *kohen* should not read [in the Torah] after another, because this might cast a suspicion on the first. [The assumption would be that the second *kohen* received an *aliyah* simply because the first *kohen* was tainted. . . . And who would suspect him? Those that remain in the synagogue [until the completion of the Torah reading (see Rashi)]. They see [that only seven people were called to the Torah, inclusive of the first *kohen* (Rashi). Thus, it is evident that the first *kohen* was considered equal to the others]. It must be, then, those who go out of the synagogue [before the *Keri'at HaTorah* was concluded. They may presume that

an additional person was called to the Torah because of the problems with the first *Kohen*] (*Gittin* 59b).

The *Peri Chadash* astutely noted that even prior to the conclusion of the *Keri'at HaTorah* it may be evident that the status of the first *kohen* was not impaired. Once the second *kohen* has read a portion of the Torah other than that read by the first *kohen*, it will be obvious that the status of the first *kohen* has not been questioned. Otherwise, the first portion should have been repeated. The *Peri Chadash*, therefore, concluded that perhaps it was not necessary for each person who received an *aliyah* to read a different portion of the Torah. The custom may have been to repeat the Torah readings. Consequently, only those who remained in the synagogue till the completion of the *Keri'at HaTorah* were able to assess the status of the first *kohen* by the total number of people called to the Torah (*Mayyim Chayyim, Gittin* 59b).

Of interest is the motivation of the Sages to prohibit the *aliyah* of a second *kohen* simply because people who leave the synagogue might depart with erroneous assumptions. Indeed, this concern was the basis for enacting *berachot* for each person who received an *aliyah*. Originally only two people recited *berachot* at *Keri'at HaTorah*: the first person prior to the reading, and the second person subsequent to the conclusion of the reading. *Berachot* were instituted because of those who either came to the synagogue in the midst of *Keri'at HaTorah* or those who departed prior to its completion. The latter might erroneously assume that *Keri'at HaTorah* lacked a final *berachah*, while the former might presume that it lacked an introductory *berachah*. To mitigate against such errors, *berachot* were instituted for all (*Megillah* 21a–b; see Rashi).

Some rationale must be presumed as to why the sages instituted changes in *Halachah* to dispel false impressions among people who did not even deem it necessary to hear the *Keri'at HaTorah*. A simple resolution would have been to enact a rule that all must hear the entire *Keri'at HaTorah*.

The Talmud says (*Bava Kamma* 82a): "[The original decree of the early prophets was] that one man should read three verses or that three men should read three verses, corresponding to *Kohanim*, *Levi'im* and *Yisraelim*. Ezra then came and ordained that three men should be called up to read [in the Torah] and that ten verses should be read."

According to the second version of the original decree, it is not clear how many verses were actually read. It could mean either that each read one verse, totaling three verses, or that each read three verses, totaling nine verses. The *Nimmukei Yosef* (Commentary on the Rif, *Bava Kamma*, chap. 7) explicitly describes the latter interpretation, which apparently was derived from the Rif, who cites: "Three persons, three, three verses" (ibid.).

The consideration of the *Nimmukei Yosef* may have been the Mishnah (*Megillah* 23b) which rules that *Keri'at HaTorah* requires the reading of a minimum of three verses corresponding to *Torah, Nevi'im, Ketuvin* (see 24a, R. Assi). Thus, there is no instance of *Keri'at HaTorah* with less than three verses. As a result, the second version of the original format of *Keri'at HaTorah* (*Bava Kamma* 82a) must mean that each person read a minimum of three verses, totaling nine altogether.

Of interest is that the rationale presented in *Megillah* for reading three verses is different from the motivation presented in *Bava Kamma*. The *Turei Even* (*Megillah* 24a) notes this distinction but discounts its significance by suggesting that there is no difference between them. Both represent alternative sources by distinct sages.

Yet a nuance of importance may be discerned. *Torah, Nevi'im,* and *Ketuvim* relate to Scripture, not people. *Kohanim, Levi'im,* and *Yisraelim* refer to people, not verses. When the Talmud discussed the minimum number of verses to be read, the source presented is *Torah, Nevi'im, Ketuvim*. When, however, the second version in *Bava Kamma* intended to indicate that the original form of *Keri'at HaTorah* had more than one person, but, rather, three, it was necessary to utilize the concept of *Kohanim, Levi'im, Yisraelim*.

It is suggested that even according to the second version

there was no requirement to read nine different verses. It was conceivable the *levi* and the *yisrael* read the same portion read by the *kohen*. The only reason why the second person read three verses rather than one was because *Keri'at HaTorah* requires a minimum of three verses. But whether the reading of the second had to be distinct from the first is not noted. The second version merely increased the number of people called to the Torah—not the number of different verses read. Even when more than three were called to the Torah, the practice of repeating sections may have prevailed.

As a result of the repetitive nature of *Keri'at HaTorah*, some did not feel the necessity to remain in the synagogue during the entire Torah reading. Thus, some came late and others departed early. Since such activity was totally in accord with *Halachah*, the sages enacted a variety of decrees (i.e., *berachot* for each *aliyah*, prohibition of a *kohen* following a *kohen*) to forestall erroneous assumptions.

Indeed, the Talmud states (*Berachot* 8a) that in the time between *aliyot* (*bain gavrah legavrah*), R. Abbahu left the synagogue. The *Chav'ot Yair* noted that R. Abbahu was involved in communal affairs and, therefore, was impelled on numerous occasions to leave the synagogue for such activity, even in the middle of *Keri'at HaTorah*. However, he would not depart in the middle of the reading but would wait for the period when the Torah was rolled up and another person was called to the Torah (Responsum 152). This theory is not necessary. R. Abbahu may have left the synagogue simply because they were repeating the Torah reading. Yet he would not depart in the middle of *Keri'at HaTorah*.

For this reason the Talmud may have permitted minors (and even women) to receive *aliyot* (*Megillah* 23a, 24a). They were called to the Torah after the minimum Torah verses were read. Since they repeated what others had already read, the sages saw no reason to exclude them. Also, they may not have chanted any *berachot* at all.

The *Beit Yosef* cites the *Shibbolai Haleket* that the reason seven people are called to the Torah on Shabbat is that someone who failed to attend synagogue services during the seven days of the week, thereby not hearing the *Barechu,* might be attentive to those who receive *aliyot* and thus meet his requirement (*Tur, Orach Chayyim* 282).

The *Penai Yehoshua* poses the question that such a theory appears to be in conflict with the (above-stated) original custom wherein only the first and last persons called to the Torah recited *berachot.* To this he suggests that even though originally only two people chanted the *berachot,* maybe all seven recited the *Barechu* (Commentary, *Megillah* 23a).

The role of the *ba'al koreh,* the official reader for *Keri'at HaTorah,* was enacted subsequent to the Talmudic era. Prior to this, blind persons could not receive an *aliyah* because they were unable to personally read from the Torah (*Mas'at Binyamin,* Responsum 62).

Rabbenu Asher contends that the *ba'al koreh* was not instituted as a means of preventing embarrassment to those unable to read in the Torah. Since the lack of an *aliyah* is not a sin, such people would simply be excluded from being called to the Torah. Should they desire an *aliyah,* they would be obliged to acquire the necessary knowledge. The concern was, rather, the sheer difficulty in mastering the cantillation. The Sages were apprehensive that communal discord might emerge if general presumptions of proficiency were questioned by local synagogue leaders. As a result, an official *ba'al koreh* was established as a vehicle to promote synagogue harmony (*Megillah* chap. 3).

Though Rabbenu Asher (ibid.) mandates those called to the Torah to silently read each word of the *parashah,* the *Mas'at Binyamin* rules that it is not necessary (*op cit.*).

Addendum

It is of interest to note that even the *Mishnah Berurah* (op. cit.), who insists that one must hear each word of *Keri'at HaTorah,* does not maintain that *Keri'at HaTorah* is a personal obligation upon each Jew. In his commentary *Be'ur Halachah* (*Orach Chayyim* 135:14), he notes that the reason why some authorities contend that one should not bring a *Sefer Torah* to a prison is, perhaps, that their case related to a situation where less than a *minyan* were incarcerated. The concern was to gather a *minyan* in the prison to enable the few prisoners to pray and hear *Keri'at HaTorah*. In such a situation, "wherein an individual cannot attend synagogue services, there is no obligation upon him to hear *Keri'at HaTorah*." In other words, *Keri'at HaTorah* is a communal rather than a personal obligation. Yet according to the *Mishnah Berurah*, the obligation devolves upon all who are able to attend synagogue services. Indeed, total attention is required of those who are present during *Keri'at HaTorah*. R. Yosef Rosen, moreover, specifically rules that when there is a congregation (which maintains full services), an individual has no obligation to hear *Keri'at HaTorah*. If, however, there is no congregation, each individual is mandated to establish a *minyan* for the *Keri'at HaTorah*. This rule, he notes, does not refer to the specific songs *(shirot)* of the Torah which each individual is personally obligated to hear *(Tzafenat Pane'ach*, Commentary on Rambam, part 1, *Hilchot Tefillah*, chap. 12, law 5; see Yerushalmi, conclusion of tractate *Megillah*).

(This theory is not presented to suggest definitive Halachic practice. It is merely noted as an insight into the nature of *Keri'at HaTorah* that is generally not noted by current Halachic authorities.)

THE PURPOSE OF *KERI'AT* HATORAH

It is necessary to analyze the pragmatic purpose of *Keri'at HaTorah*. Why was it enacted? What purpose does it serve? If *Keri'at HaTorah* is a form of public Torah study *(Talmud Torah)*, why was it not ordained to be conducted each day? Are not Jews mandated to learn Torah each day? The *berachot* chanted at *Keri'at HaTorah* are different from those recited each day by Jews prior to Torah study. This suggests that *Keri'at HaTorah* has a nuance of distinction that sets it apart qualitatively from the personal obligation of each Jew to learn Torah.

Rabbenu Tam *(Rosh Hashanah* 33a) contends that the blessings before and after *Keri'at HaTorah* have no relationship to the *mitzvah* of learning Torah, for even if a person chanted his personal *Birchat HaTorah* (prior to learning Torah), he is still obliged upon receiving an *aliyah* to chant the special *berachot* of *Keri'at HaTorah*. The *Tur* (*Orach Chayyim* 139) quotes the decision of his father, Rabbenu Asher, and this is the Halachah, that a person who comes late to synagogue services, chants the *Birchat HaTorah,* and then is called for an *aliyah* before he has an opportunity to learn any Torah at all is still obliged to chant the specific *berachot* required at *Keri'at HaTorah*. Thus it is evident that *Keri'at HaTorah* may not be classified as having the same status as Torah study.

The Mishnah rules that *Keri'at HaTorah* may not take place unless a *minyan* (quorum of ten Jews) is present. The Gemara provides the rationale by contending that *Keri'at HaTorah* is a form of *kedushah* (sanctification of the Holy Name), and there is a general rule that all matters of *kedushah* require a *minyan* (*Megillah,* 23b). The whole basis for the requirement of a *minyan* for *Keri'at HaTorah* is its status as a form of *kedushah*. What is not immediately apparent is why *Keri'at HaTorah* is categorized as a form of *kedushah,* while the personal study of Torah is not vested with such a status. One may assume that even if a rabbi were teaching Torah to a thousand students, this would not transform the Torah study to a status of *kedushah*. Wherein does *Keri'at HaTorah* differ from personal Torah study? The logical distinction derives from the fact that *Keri'at HaTorah* must be performed with a *Sefer Torah*—i.e., it is the presence of the *Sefer Torah* that vests the process with the aura of *kedushah*. What then is the function of *Keri'at HaTorah*?

The *Tur* (*Orach Chayyim* 47) discusses the various *berachot* that must be chanted prior to Torah study each day. He then notes:

There is [yet] another *berachah* over Torah; namely *Asher bachar banu* [translation: "which selected us (the Jewish people) . . . and gave us his Torah"]. When chanting this blessing one should have intention [*kavvanah*] for the revelation on Mount Sinai wherein He selected us from all the nations, brought us to Mount Sinai and made heard His words . . . and gave us His holy Torah which is our life and treasure.

The *Bach* contends that the *Tur* is actually providing a solution to a major Halachic problem: namely, why does Torah study require more *berachot* than any other *mitzvah*? Prior to the performance of any *mitzvah* only one *berachah* is chanted; that *berachah* is classified as a *birchat hamitzvah* (a blessing chanted before the observance of a *mitzvah*). Why is it necessary to chant the concluding *Asher bachar banu* blessing? Once the Jew has concluded his first *berachah* (the second blessing is considered by many to be an extension of the first), why mandate an extraneous *berachah*? To this the *Bach* suggests the following:

The first *berachah* is a typical *birchat hamitzvah* chanted before the observance of any *mitzvah*. The second *berachah* (*Asher bachar banu*) is not a *birchat hamitzvah*. It is a form of thanksgiving and praise for receiving Torah on Mount Sinai. Scripture states: "Only take heed to thyself . . . lest thou forget the things which thine eyes have seen, and lest they depart from thy heart all the days of thy life, but bring them to the knowledge of thy children and thy children's children. The day that thou stoodest before thy God at Horeb . . ." (Deuteronomy 4:7–10). Thus, concludes the *Bach*, the second *berachah* is a means of observing the Biblical mandate of never forgetting the revelation of Mount Sinai (*Orach Chayyim* 47).

Based upon this theory of the *Bach*, it is possible to clarify the *raison d'être* of *Keri'at HaTorah*. Since *Asher bachar banu* is the basic *berachah* prior to the reading of the Torah, it is logical to assume that this blessing relates to the prime purpose of *Keri'at HaTorah*, namely, to keep the revelation at Mount Sinai alive in the minds of the Jewish people. The Ramban, in his commentary on Deuteronomy, specifically states that the above-noted verse explicitly prohibits forgetting the revelation and is one of the 613 primary *mitzvot*. (Those who dispute with the Ramban contend that this verse does not relate specifically to the revelation but to a general prohibition against forgetting Torah.)

Moshe Rabbenu wished to ensure that Israel would cherish its holy legacy, the Torah. How was he to do this? The most viable means of guaranteeing the Torah was to establish a rite that would vividly emulate the revelation, the source of all

Torah. The holy *Sefer Torah,* which had been acquired at Sinai and possessed its own *kedushah,* was the object that more than anything else symbolized the revelation; nothing could have been better suited to a rite emulating the *kedushah* of Mount Sinai. Thus it becomes apparent why Moshe Rabbenu decreed that the Torah should be read on Shabbat: in addition to being the first day after his death, Shabbat was, according to tradition, the day on which the Torah had been given; and thus the very day chosen for the Torah reading was a dramatic reminder of the original gift of Torah. Since the *Keri'at HaTorah* was not a form of public Torah study but a means of emulating Sinai, it is understandable why it is classified as a form of *kedushah* and requires the presence of a *minyan.* On Mount Sinai the Torah was not given to individuals. It was granted to a people, *Kelal Yisrael,* and all of them, therefore, were in attendance. Revelation, the ultimate source of our national soul and pride, is the true seed of *kedushah.* The blessing *Asher bachar banu* does not relate to the private obligations of the individual Jew. It is an affirmation that Jews are involved in Torah only because they are members of *Kelal Yisrael.* Membership in the group is what provides the individual with his entrée to Torah. *Kedushat Yisrael* is derived from *Kedushat HaTorah.* Thus *Keri'at HaTorah* is a means of implanting the belief that the sanctity of the Jewish people is interrelated with the sanctity of Torah. It is for this reason that *Keri'at HaTorah* is a communal *mitzvah* rather than a personal obligation. It was probably to emphasize the element of *kedushah* that the *Barechu* (introduction) prior to the blessing was instituted, as a ritual that publicly acknowledges the status of *kedushah* inherent in the process.

In addition to the points already mentioned, the preceding analysis presents a clear, cogent meaning for the Talmud's statement that "whosoever writes a *Sefer Torah* is comparable to having received it from Mount Sinai" (*Menachot* 30a). Perhaps the Talmud means exactly what it says, directing our attention to the purpose of the *mitzvah.* A *Sefer Torah* is not just a text for study, it is a simulation of Sinai. It is an object of *kedushah* and should only be utilized within an aura of *kedushah.*

All this makes it possible to understand the development of the custom of donating a *Sefer Torah* to a synagogue after the process of writing it was completed. The custom was not just a means of providing safe storage for a holy object. It had two interrelated purposes:

1. To emulate the role of Moshe Rabbenu; just as he wrote a *Sefer Torah* and granted it to the community, so too does each Jew.

2. As R. Shlomo Kluger (op. cit.) noted, the purpose of writing a *Sefer Torah* was to manifest appreciation for the power of scholars to create *kedushah*. What greater manifestation of *kedushah* could there be than to use a *Sefer Torah* for *Keri'at HaTorah*, the public simulation of the *kedushah* of revelation. Man is able to create *kedushah* primarily because of the *kedushah* of Mount Sinai. The *Sefer Torah*, as an object of *kedushah*, written to demonstrate the power of sages to confer *kedushah*, is utilized in a process, *Keri'at HaTorah*, that is a dramatic reenactment of the source of *kedushah* (revelation), and should be stored in a house of *kedushah*, the synagogue. As this demonstrates, Jewish customs are not empty rituals. They are based upon firm theological principles which enhance the glorification of our faith.

3

Why There Is No *Berachah* for Writing a *Sefer Torah*

The Biblical *mitzvah* of writing a *Sefer Torah* differs from other *mitzvot* in that there is no *berachah* appended to it. Why is this so? Why should the Biblical *mitzvah* of writing a *Sefer Torah* be different from, for example, eating *matzah*, wearing *tefillin*, or sounding the *shofar*? In each of the latter three cases, one chants a ritual *berachah* prior to performing the *mitzvah*.

A suggested resolution relates to the format and purpose of *birchat hamitzvot*. A *berachah* is an introductory statement preceding an action which is a *mitzvah*. Thus, one chants a *berachah* prior to the sounding of the *shofar* or the reading of the *Megillah*; the performance of the action subsequent to the *berachah* constitutes the fulfillment of the *mitzvah*. In such instances the *berachah* serves the following purposes.

1. It emphasizes that the subsequent action is formally recognized as a *mitzvah* and is, therefore, being performed with proper intention *(kavvanah)*. (Thus, authorities suggest that once a *mitzvah* is completed there is no valid reason for the chanting of a *berachah*.)
2. It is a formal recognition that the *mitzvah* to be performed was not invented by Moshe (or by others or by us) but is a dictate of the Almighty. Rabbinical *Mitzvot* also necessitate a *berachah* to acknowledge the obligation to heed the rules of rabbinic Torah sages *(Responsa Ketav Sofer, Orach Chayyim,*

34

21). In other words, the *berachah* is an ideological commitment to the sanctity of the source of *mitzvot* prior to the actual performance.

As both of the preceding reasons indicate, an action follows the *berachah*.

The *mitzvah* of writing a *Sefer Torah* is not fulfilled until the *Sefer Torah* is completely written and assessed to be correct. Thus, the *mitzvah* is not the process of writing but, rather, its completion. Someone who writes half of a *Sefer Torah* does not acquire half of a *mitzvah*. It is only after the last letter is written that the object is transformed into a *Sefer Torah* and acquires a status of *kedushah*. The writing process is merely a conditional aspect of preparing the object of a *mitzvah;* it is not the *mitzvah* itself.

This understanding of the *mitzvah* of writing a *Sefer Torah* is suggested by the terminology of the Rambam, who rules: "It is a Biblical command for every single Jew to write a *Sefer Torah* for himself. . . . If he wrote it by hand, it is comparable to having received it from Mount Sinai, and if he does not know how to write [the *Sefer Torah*], others write for him" (Rambam, *Hilchot Sefer Torah*, chap. 7, law 1).

Note the terminology used by the Rambam in this passage. If the writing process were an aspect of the *mitzvah,* the Rambam would have stated that the *mitzvah* should be performed *"by* himself" rather than *"for* himself." "By himself" would connote the personal involvement that is necessary in the performance of a *mitzvah,* but "for himself," the phrase actually utilized by the Rambam, merely suggests ownership and/or ultimate possession. Similarly, the Rambam said that if one does not know how to write a *Sefer Torah*, "others" should write it. His use of the vague term "others," rather than a specific requirement that it be written by one's agent and/or surrogate *(shaliach),* suggests that a formal surrogate is not necessary. Lastly, the Rambam discusses the writing process in a conditional context: "If he wrote it." But if the writing of the *Sefer Torah* is the basic *mitzvah,* he should have affirmatively and decisively stated that one should write the *Sefer Torah* by hand. It is a general principle that all *mitzvot* should preferably be performed by oneself rather than by means of a surrogate. Also, the fact that the Rambam in *Sefer HaMitzvot* (18) rules that one who cannot write a *Sefer Torah* may acquire the *mitzvah* by purchase surely substantiates the position that the writing process is not part of the *mitzvah*. Otherwise it would be impossible to acquire the *mitzvah* once the writing process was concluded.*

The *Sefer HaChinnuch* (*mitzvah* 613) notes "that every Jewish male is commanded to have a *Sefer Torah*." Thus, the *Chinnuch* does not state that the *mitzvah* is to write a *Sefer Torah*. The writing process is merely the preparatory condition for the final *mitzvah*, but not the *mitzvah* itself.

Thus, while there are a variety of regulations pertaining to the writing of a *Sefer Torah*, it is the end product and not the process that constitutes the *mitzvah*: i.e., a completed *Sefer Torah* written according to specific rules. Only when the writing process has been completed is the object transformed into a *Sefer Torah*. In other words, possession without action is itself the *mitzvah*. (Previous discussion has demonstrated that continual possession is not necessary.)

As a result, no special *berachah* was ordained for this *mitzvah*. As previously noted, a *berachah* only precedes the performance of an action which is itself the fulfillment of a *mitzvah*. A *berachah* does not precede the observance of an involuntary, spontaneous, inactive *mitzvah*. Similarly, *berachot* are not mandated for

---

*R. Amram Blum (*Responsa Beit Sha'arim, Yoreh De'ah*, part II, responsum 365) invokes such textual comments upon the Rambam to support the position that an agent and/or surrogate (*shaliach*) need not be formally appointed to write a *Sefer Torah*. In responsum 366, R. Blum forestalls a possible challenge to this theory by explaining why Rama ruled that the purchaser of a *Sefer Torah* is not vested with the *mitzvah* (*Yoreh De'ah* 270); Rama did not believe that writing the *Sefer Torah* is an intrinsic aspect of the *mitzvah* but understood the Scriptural mandate *Kitvo lachem*—"Write for yourselves"—as suggesting that ownership is necessary during the writing process.

negative prohibitions. For example, one does not make a *berachah* for not violating the Shabbat. Thus, since no action is required (and the writing process is not a *mitzvah*), no *berachah* is mandated.

This presentation clarifies yet another difficult Talmudic passage. It is recorded *(Gittin* 52a) that an *Apotropos* (the executor of a minor's estate) was mandated to acquire a *Sefer Torah*, *tefillin*, and *mezuzot* for the child under his jurisdiction. The Rambam states that these were acquired "even though they [the children] were not obligated in any of the *mitzvot* except for the purpose of *chinnuch*" (Rambam, *Hilchot Nachalot*, chap. 11. law 10). There appears to be a qualitative difference between *chinnuch* as pertaining to a *Sefer Torah* and *chinnuch* as relating to *tefillin* and *mezuzot*. In the latter two instances the minor may continue to utilize the ritual objects acquired for him during his minor status when he attains his legal majority. He may wear the same *tefillin* and use the same *mezuzot* as an adult that he utilized as a child. This is a classic example of *chinnuch* as practical experience for children in *mitzvot* which they will be obligated to observe upon maturity. In regard to a *Sefer Torah*, however, other considerations are operative. If the *mitzvah* were to actually write a *Sefer Torah*, then a minor who wrote a *Sefer Torah* would not be able to utilize it when he became an adult. Since a *Sefer Torah* written by a minor is not valid for usage, he would be mandated upon maturity to write another *Sefer Torah*. If a minor cannot write a *Sefer Torah*, he certainly cannot appoint a surrogate to accomplish this task for him, for there is a general rule that one cannot appoint an agent to do something in one's behalf that one is legally prohibited from doing oneself. Thus, this case differs from the general pattern of *chinnuch* as a practical experience in *mitzvot* with the rituals utilized in accordance with Halachah (i.e., the same acts would be deemed the fulfillment of a *mitzvah* if performed by an adult). *Chinnuch* must be an exposure to a practical future religious activity.

According to the view that the writing process is not the *mitzvah*, but merely a condition to crystallize the *mitzvah*, all difficulties relating to the above case may be resolved. The *apotropos* writes or has someone write a *Sefer Torah* for the minor. The minor owns the *Sefer Torah*. It is not necessary for the *Sofer* to have been formally appointed to the task as an agent of the owner. It suffices that a *Sefer Torah* was written correctly in behalf of someone. In consequence, the minor upon attaining maturity may definitely use the *Sefer Torah* to fulfill his *mitzvah*. Thus, the *Sefer Torah* is on an equal status with *tefillin* and *mezuzot*.

An alternate rationale for the lack of a *berachah* for the *mitzvah* of writing a *Sefer Torah* may be derived from the following rule stated by the Rambam:

> Whenever there is a *mitzvah* that has yet another command attached to it, one does not make a *berachah* until the final command is fulfilled. For example, one does not make a *berachah* upon making a *sukkah, lulav, shofar, tzitzit, tefillin,* or *mezuzah.* One rather makes a *berachah* when one sits in the *sukkah,* shakes the *lulav,* blows the *shofar,* wears the *tzitzit,* and places the *mezuzah* on the doorpost.
> (Rambam, *Hilchot Berachot*, chap. 11, law 8)

If the purpose of writing a *Sefer Torah* is to learn Torah (Rabbenu Asher) or to emulate the *kedushah* of Sinai, then the *mitzvah* is not completed until one actually studies the *Sefer Torah* or uses it to manifest the *kedushah* of Sinai by the process of *Keri'at HaTorah*. In other words, the reason or rationale of the *mitzvah* may itself become a vital, integral aspect of the *mitzvah*. One who merely writes a *Sefer Torah* and does not use it is comparable to one who builds a *sukkah* and does not dwell within it.

There is a precedent for the concept that the rationale of a *mitzvah* must be operative in order for the *mitzvah* to be performed. The Bible states: "You shall dwell in the *sukkot* for seven days, all that are native-born in Israel shall dwell in *sukkot*. So that your generations may know that in *sukkot* did I make the children of Israel dwell when I brought them out from the land of Egypt; I am God, your Lord" (Leviticus 23:42–43).

The *Bach* (*Orach Chayyim* 625) suggests that since Scripture presents the rationale for the *mitzvah* of *sukkot*, it is possible that one does not fulfill the *mitzvah* properly unless consideration for the motivation of the *mitzvah* is present in one's mind at the moment of performing it.

HaGaon R. Yitzchak Hutner, *z. l.*, my Rosh Yeshivah, contended that every aspect of love has a reason substantiating the basis for such love. As a result, the *mitzvah* of loving one's friend (Leviticus 19:18) must have a rationale justifying the emotion. He contends that the *mitzvah* is not merely to love one's friend who is a Jew but to love him because he is a Jew. The reason for the love becomes part of the *mitzvah*. (The verse is interpreted as follows: "and you shall love your friend" [*lere'acha*]—because he is *rey-acha*.) Thus it is suggested that if one loves another Jew but does not know that he is Jewish, the *mitzvah* is not performed correctly. On the other hand, the Biblical prohibition of not hating one's brother (Leviticus 19:17) is interpreted to mean: not to hate him because of his brotherhood in the faith. It is the bond of brotherhood that prohibits the hatred. Thus, should one hate another person and not know that he is Jewish, it is possible that such hatred is not a violation of a Biblical prohibition (see *Pachad Yitzchak, Pesach,* part I, *Ma'amar* 8).

Though the above analysis is unique and not representative of the mainstream of interpretation for such *mitzvot*, it is presented as a stark illustration of how the reason for a *mitzvah* may at times be utilized as part of the *mitzvah* itself.

As for the *mitzvah* of writing a *Sefer Torah*, Scripture itself clearly maintains that its motivation is to teach Torah to the children of Israel (Deuteronomy 31:19, 22). Thus, it is possible that the *berachot* of *Keri'at HaTorah* may be the true *berachot* for the *mitzvah* of writing a *Sefer Torah;* for reading and/or learning the *Sefer Torah* may be the culmination of the *mitzvah* of writing a *Sefer Torah*. The active utilization of the Torah occurs during the process of Keri'at HaTorah. For this reason, no *berachah* was mandated prior to this process. It is comparable to making a *berachah* only when one actually dwells in a *sukkah*. (This

certainly gives added impetus to the position of the Lubavitcher Rebbe, *Shlita*, that each person who has an *aliyah* is vested
with ownership of the *Sefer Torah*, see chapter 16.)

R. Ephraim Zalman Margolit, in his classic codes of *Keri'at
HaTorah*, notes that upon completion of a *Sefer Torah*, some
follow the custom of chanting the *Shehecheyanu* blessing the first
time that they receive an *aliyah* in the new Torah. Since some
authorities disagree with the need for such a blessing, he
suggests that it may be chanted if one is wearing a new
garment. This way the *berachah* relates to both the Torah and the
garment (see *Sha'ar Ephraim*, *sha'ar* 4, law 34).

In his commentary *Pitchei Sha'arim* (loc. cit), it is clarified that
the moment of *aliyah* to the Torah does not create the *mitzvah* of
writing a *Sefer Torah*. That *mitzvah* occurred prior to *Keri'at
HaTorah*. As a result, one certainly may chant the *Shehecheyanu
berachah* upon completion of the review process which verifies
the accuracy of the *Sefer Torah*. Yet it is permissible to withhold
the *berachah* until one has an *aliyah*, for "the individual is joyous
that he was privileged to read in his own *Sefer Torah* and also
make a blessing relating to the making of the *Sefer Torah*."

However, according to the proponents of the *minhag* that
limited the chanting of the *Shehecheyanu berachah* to *Keri'at
HaTorah*, it appears that there is a close interrelationship between the *mitzvah* of writing a *Sefer Torah* and *Keri'at HaTorah*.
Indeed, the commentary *Sha'arei Rachamim* (ibid.) notes that
one is mandated to give a person an *aliyah* to read in a new *Sefer
Torah* on the first Shabbat after he completes it.

The reason for such customs may be as previously stated.
Keri'at HaTorah may be the culmination of the *mitzvah* of writing
a *Sefer Torah*. As a result, any *berachah* that relates somehow to
the *mitzvah* of writing a *Sefer Torah* should be appended to the
process of *Keri'at HaTorah*.

Those authorities who maintain that the *Shehecheyanu berachah* need not await *Keri'at HaTorah* may be of the opinion that
the total *mitzvah* is performed even though one does not learn
Torah from the *Sefer Torah*. Yet it is of interest to note that even
such scholars do not contend that it is wrong to prolong the

berachah till *Keri'at HaTorah.* In other words, even if *Keri'at HaTorah* is not the culmination of the *mitzvah* of writing a *Sefer Torah,* it does relate in some way to the *mitzvah.* It may be considered in the category of a *kiyyum hamitzvah* (i.e., a process not obligated but certainly within the spirit of the *mitzvah*). That *Keri'at HaTorah* relates in some way to the *mitzvah* of writing a *Sefer Torah* is unquestionable.

4

Women and the *Mitzvah* of Writing a *Sefer Torah*

The Rambam rules that "every single Jewish *male*" has a Biblical *mitzvah* to write a *Sefer Torah* (*Laws of Sefer Torah*, chap. 7, law 1). The obvious inference is that women are excluded from the *mitzvah*. Indeed, the Rambam leaves no possible doubt as to his intention by specifically recording in the *Sefer HaMitzvot* that *mitzvah* 18 (the *mitzvah* of writing a *Sefer Torah*) is not applicable to women (*Sefer HaMitzvot*, conclusion of section on positive commandments).

Yet no reason is presented for the exclusion of women from the *mitzvah*. Writing and possessing a *Sefer Torah* is not comparable to, for example, the *mitzvah* of *tefillin*, which is not observed on Shabbat, holidays, or at night. Women are exempt from *tefillin* because they are not required to perform *mitzvot* which must be observed only within a specific time reference. The *mitzvah* of writing a *Sefer Torah*, however, has no time dimension. It may be observed at any and all times. If so, why are women excluded from the *mitzvah*?

The *Shagot Aryeh* (responsum 35) outlines three possible reasons for the exclusion of women and then challenges the validity of each of them.

1. Rabbenu Asher ruled that learning Torah is the purpose of the *mitzvah* of writing a *Sefer Torah*. Since women are exempt from the *mitzvah* of learning Torah, there is no reason to obligate them to write a *Sefer Torah*.

2. Women are exempt from performing many of the *mitzvot*. Since the *Sefer Torah* includes all of the *mitzvot*, they should not be obligated to write a *Sefer Torah*. (In other words, why require them to write something that they are not commanded to observe?)

3. A woman may not serve as a scribe to write a *Sefer Torah*. Since women cannot perform the writing process, they should be excluded from the *mitzvah*.

The *Shagot Aryeh* refutes each of these points with the following arguments:

1. Women are required to learn the *mitzvot* applicable to them. Indeed, it has been Halachically decided that they may voluntarily assume the obligation to chant the *Birchat Ha-Torah*. As a result, they certainly are involved in the *mitzvah* of learning Torah and should be mandated to write a *Sefer Torah*.

2. The logical extension of the reasoning that women are exempt from writing a *Sefer Torah* because they are not required to perform certain *mitzvot* would also exempt most Jewish men from the *mitzvah*. Many *mitzvot* are only applicable to *kohanim* or to a *kohen gadol*. Some *mitzvot* relate only to kings. Are non-*kohanim* exempt from writing a *Sefer Torah* simply because it contains *mitzvot* that they are not commanded to observe?

3. Although women may not write *mezuzot*, they are required to have *mezuzot* on their doorposts. Just as exemption from the writing process does not exclude them from the *mitzvah* of *mezuzot*, it should not exclude them in the case of a *Sefer Torah*.

On the basis of the preceding analysis, the *Shagot Aryeh* concludes that there is no logical foundation for the Rambam's exemption of women from the *mitzvah*.

R. Yosef Dov Ber Soloveitchik (*Responsa Beit Halevi*, no. 6) suggests that women are excluded from the *mitzvah* simply because they are not obligated to learn Torah. The fact that women need to learn the *mitzvot* applicable to them does not place them in the same category as men. Indeed, there is a major qualitative distinction differentiating the roles of women and men in Torah study.

Men are mandated to learn even the *mitzvot* that they are not required to observe. This means that a man who is not a *kohen*, and therefore is not obligated to observe the laws pertaining to *kohanim*, is still required to learn the Torah and *mitzvot* of *kohanim*. Torah learning is all-inclusive and prevails even in instances where observance is not required. Men are mandated to learn all the *mitzvot* of the Torah. Women, however, have no obligation to learn those *mitzvot* which are not applicable for practical observance. As a result, their scope of Torah learning is quite limited. Since the purpose of the *mitzvah* of writing a *Sefer Torah* is not the observance of *mitzvot* but the learning of Torah, women, with their limited obligations, are exempt from the *mitzvah*. Men, however, are directly involved in all *mitzvot*—because of their mandate to learn all facets of Torah.

The *Beit Halevi* in his commentary on the Pentateuch (*Parashat Mishpatim*) delineates a further fine distinction between the obligations of men and women in the sphere of Torah study. He notes that Torah education has a twofold aim: the pursuit of Torah knowledge as a means to better observance of commandments and as an end in itself.

An elaboration of this distinction is as follows: To be a good Jew—to carefully and scrupulously follow the dictates of our religion—it is necessary to be well acquainted with many of its laws and customs. Indeed, it is written that an ignoramus cannot be a pious person. This is quite understandable, for a person who is ignorant of Judaism certainly cannot know whether he is doing something right or wrong. It is, moreover, practically impossible to observe the Shabbat if one is ignorant of the intricate, detailed laws of this holy day. Thus, Torah study serves as the vehicle to stimulate the observance of *mitzvot*. Women are involved in this facet of Torah study.

Yet there is another important aspect to the study of Torah—

the obligation to study Torah for its own sake. This aspect of Torah education is not a means of observing commandments but a *mitzvah* in itself. Just as *kashrut* and putting on *tefillin* are commandments, so too is the study of Torah. This obligation is incumbent upon all Jewish men, including those who consider themselves grand masters in all aspects of the Law. Even a person who feels that he knows the entire Torah is still obligated to learn Torah. The Talmud portrays this concept when it relates that a *tanna* asked whether someone who was well versed in all aspects of the Torah was free from the obligation to study it. The answer presented was that if one could find a period of time which was neither a part of the day nor a portion of the night, only then would he be absolved of all requirements to learn Torah (*Menachot* 99b).

It is interesting to note that there is a great practical difference between the two approaches to the study of Torah. If Torah study were simply a means of acquiring the technical knowledge necessary for an observant Jew, then it would, perhaps, be possible to free oneself from the obligation to learn by retaining the services of a scholar who could outline everything one needed to know. However, since men must study Torah for its own sake, doing this would not be valid. Just as the rabbi's act of putting on *tefillin* or observing the Shabbat does not in any way free others from these *mitzvot,* so too the rabbi's intense scholarship does not in any way affect the requirement of others to spend a portion of their time learning Torah. Thus the role of men in the *mitzvah* of Torah study is categorically different from the role of women. Women are merely involved in Torah laws applicable for their own observance. They are concerned with the end product of practical, applied Torah, but men are involved in the process of learning Torah for its own sake.

This extension of the *Beit Halevi's* theory may be utilized as an additional rationale for exempting women from the *mitzvah* of writing a *Sefer Torah*. According to Rabbenu Asher, the purpose of the *mitzvah* is to learn Torah. Women may be involved in learning practical Torah concepts but have no *mitzvah* to continue learning those ideas that they already have mastered for the observance of *mitzvot*. Thus, even regard to specific *mitzvot* that women are required to observe, such as *kashrut* or Shabbat, they are not charged with a *mitzvah* to engage in the profundities of the concepts. In other words, Torah study per se is not within their mandated scope. Thus, they are limited even in regard to the *mitzvot* that are applicable to them. Since the purpose of the *mitzvah* is the process of learning Torah, however, it is understandable why they are exempt.

There is a third solution to the problem of why women were excluded from the *mitzvah* of writing and possessing a *Sefer Torah*.

Rabbenu Asher notes that the purpose of the *mitzvah* of having a *Sefer Torah* is to learn Torah. In other words, the *Sefer Torah* is to be used as a text to facilitate Torah study. Yet a careful reading of the Biblical mandate suggests a nuance generally not noted by the commentaries. The Bible at no time states that the purpose is to learn Torah. The Scripture, rather, says: "and teach it to the Children of Israel" (Deuteronomy 31:19). Indeed, the Bible says that when Moshe Rabbenu completed the Torah, "he taught it to the Children of Israel" (Deuteronomy 31:22). Thus, the purpose of the *mitzvah* is *not* to learn Torah but to teach Torah. The *Sefer Torah* was to be a text that would facilitate the teaching of Torah to *Kelal Yisrael*. The Talmud (*Kiddushin* 29b) specifically states that women are exempt from the *mitzvah* of teaching Torah. As a result, it is clear why women are exempt from the *mitzvah* of writing a *Sefer Torah*. The *Sefer Torah* was to be an aid in teaching Torah, and since women are not involved in this facet of Torah study, they are not mandated to write a *Sefer Torah*.

This formulation provides a clear distinction between the purposes of the royal *Sefer Torah* required of a king and the *Sefer Torah* mandated for the ordinary Jew. The latter may have been for teaching Torah, while the former was for learning Torah.

Somewhat of a source for this theory is the following Halachah. The *Shulchan Aruch* (*Orach Chayyim* 150:1) rules that members of a community may be coerced to acquire a *Sefer*

Torah, Nevi'im, and *Ketuvim.* The *Magen Avraham* (ibid.) notes that in our day there is also an obligation for a community to obtain a Talmud. The *Ba'er Heitev* (ibid.) reports this latter Halachah and contends that the reason is that the Talmud would facilitate anyone who wishes to learn Torah. Yet a close reading of the *Magen Avraham* reveals quite a different orientation. The *Magen Avraham* does not state that the purpose of the acquisition of a Talmud is to learn Torah or to facilitate such learning. Regarding the requirement to obtain *Ketuvim* the *Magen Avraham* notes that the purpose was so that anyone who desired might learn therein, yet of the suggestion to acquire a Talmud, the *Magen Avraham* says: *Lelamed bahem leketanim ulegedolim,* which literally means, "To teach with them to children and to adults." In other words, the purpose of the Talmud was not to learn Torah but to teach Torah. Indeed, the *Mishnah Berurah* (ibid.) quotes the exact terminology of the *Magen Avraham.*

Perhaps the theory presented is the basis for such a ruling. The *mitzvah* of writing a *Sefer Torah* was for the purpose of providing a tool for the teaching of Torah. As religious texts took the place of *Sifrei Torah,* they too were to be utilized for purposes of teaching rather than learning Torah.

This position also generates new insights into the basic formulation of the *mitzvah.*

Moshe is traditionally referred to as Rabbenu—"our Rebbe"—our teacher. This suggests that his foremost role as a leader was that as a teacher of Torah. It is for this reason, perhaps, that he instituted *Keri'at HaTorah* (Rambam, op. cit.). It was a vehicle to perpetuate his role after his death. No longer would *Kelal Yisrael* need to depend upon one man. Every community would have an opportunity to manifest public Torah study. But why was it necessary to read only in a *Sefer Torah?* Why was it not sufficient to ritualize a Torah study session during prayers? The necessity of using a *Sefer Torah* suggests that a *Sefer Torah* plays a unique role in Torah study.

The Talmud (*Sotah* 37a) contends that for each *mitzvah* there were four covenants relating to the following four integral aspects of *mitzvot*: to learn (*lilmod*), to teach (*lelamed*), to guard (*lishmor*), and to observe (*la'asot*). Commenting on this citation, the Brisker Rav (R. Yitzchak Ze'ev Soloveitchik, Bible—*Parashat Devorim*) notes that the third aspect requires definition. What, he asks, is the distinction between guarding Torah and observing Torah? Since the latter clause relates to both positive and negative commandments, guarding Torah must have a specific application. The Brisker Rav suggests that the commitment "to guard Torah" (*lishmor*) refers to the need to preserve the purity of the *Mesorah*. It is, therefore, an obligation not only to learn Torah and observe Torah and *mitzvot* but also to sustain the purity of the transmission of Torah.

This then may be the key to the establishment of *Keri'at HaTorah* and an additional reason for the *mitzvah* of writing a *Sefer Torah*. The Midrash notes that Moshe Rabbenu wrote thirteen *Sifrei Torah* on the day of his death. Each of the twelve tribes was given a *Sefer Torah*, and the thirteenth was placed in the Ark, so that if an attempt were made to falsify the Torah, the *Sefer Torah* in the Sanctuary could be brought out (to validate the issue) (*Midrash Rabbah*, Deuteronomy, *parashah* 9, *Vayelech*). Thus Moshe Rabbenu was acutely concerned with preserving the accuracy and authenticity of the Torah (see Rambam, op. cit., that Moshe Rabbenu ordained *Keri'at HaTorah*).

It may, therefore, be conjectured that *Keri'at HaTorah* was established not merely as a format for the public teaching of Torah but specifically to emphasize the purity and accuracy of Torah as exemplified by the *Sefer Torah*. The teaching of Torah must be based upon *Torat Moshe*—the *Sefer Torah* itself—to preserve Torah for future generations.

The original format must not be falsified. It must be preserved intact. Thus, *Keri'at HaTorah* was an ordinance to sustain the purity of the *Mesorah*. For this reason, perhaps, the sages did not enact the usual format of a *berachah* for *Keri'at HaTorah*. The ritual phrase *Asher kiddishanu bemitzvotav* ("which You sanctified us with Your *mitzvot*") is not chanted before *Keri'at HaTorah* because the public Torah reading is not a specific *mitzvah* but a means of sustaining the totality of Torah itself.

Since every Jew is potentially a teacher of Torah, every Jew was required to possess a personal *Sefer Torah*. Thus every Jew had a reminder that the teachings of Torah should be in accord with the content of the *Sefer Torah*.

Thus, the 613th *mitzvah* symbolizes the basic tenets of our faith. It symbolizes an appreciation of *kedushah*, a reenactment of the climate of Sinai, a means of learning, teaching, guarding, and of course, through all, observing Torah itself.

Addendum

The *Beit Halevi*'s theory (op. cit.) that men are obliged to learn even *mitzvot* that they are not required to observe, while women are only mandated to acquire knowledge that facilitates the performance of obligatory *mitzvot*, is noted by a number of Halachic authorities (see, for example, R. Shlomo Ganzfried, *Lishkat HaSofer* 1: note 3). The *Avnei Nezer* also presents this view, but adds an interesting nuance to the concept. He contends that since it is almost impossible to observe *mitzvot* without practical knowledge, the acquisition of such knowledge is categorized as the commencement of the performance of the *mitzvah*, rather than as part of the general principle of learning Torah. Thus, for women the process of learning is, in reality, an integral aspect of the observance. Hence, they are not involved in the general *mitzvah* of learning Torah (*Responsa Avnei Nezer, Yoreh De'ah*, part II, 352).

5

Kedushat HaShem and Kedushat Sefer Torah

A scribe who writes a *Sefer Torah* must manifest two specific religious concerns.

1. As he begins to write the *Sefer Torah* he must state, "This *Sefer* I am writing for the sake of the holiness of a *Sefer Torah*" (*Shulchan Aruch, Yoreh De'ah* 274:1). This concept will be referred to as *Kedushat Sefer Torah*.
2. Prior to writing each of the Holy Names (of the Almighty), which are prohibited to be erased, the scribe must say that he is writing them "for the purpose of the *Kedushah* of the Holy Name." If he fails to do so, the *Sefer Torah* is not valid for (synagogue) use (ibid., 276:1). This concept will be referred to as *Kedushat HaShem*.

Halachic authorities disagree as to whether it is sufficient for the scribe simply to think these sentiments (*machshavah*) or whether it is necessary for him to intone an oral, vocal statement.

The Rama (*Orach Chayyim* 32:19) notes that as long as the scribe vocally expresses *Kedushat Sefer Torah*, *Kedushat HaShem* need not be orally manifested. Based upon the Rama, the *Mishnah Berurah* (ibid.) rules that: (1) *Kedushat Sefer* must be vocal; (2) *Kedushat HaShem* may be an internal thought process;

50

and (3) if either of these two elements are missing, the *Sefer Torah* lacks *kedushah* and is not valid for synagogue services.

A more lenient position is expressed by R. Shlomo Ganzfried, the author of the *Kitzur Shulchan Aruch* (see the classic volume on *Sefer Torah, Keset HaSofer and Lishkat Sofer*). He notes that even *Kedushat Sefer Torah* need not be orally invoked (4:2, also 10:2–3).

Whatever the final Halachah on this specific issue, all agree that it is preferable for both *Kedushat Sefer Torah* and *Kedushat HaShem* to be vocally expressed. The above-noted debate relates only to a fait accompli wherein the scribe neglected to make such oral statements. In addition, the Halachic consensus is that if such ritual sentiments are altogether lacking, the *Sefer Torah* is invalid for synagogue use and the *mitzvah* of writing a *Sefer Torah* has not been observed.

KEDUSHAT HASHEM

A basic Talmudic source for the requirement of *Kedushat HaShem* is the following passage (*Gittin* 54b):

> A certain man appeared before R. Ammi and said to him: "In a *Sefer Torah* which I have written for So-and-So, I have not written the names of God with proper intention." R. Ammi asked him: "Who has the *Sefer Torah*?" He replied: "The purchaser." Whereupon he said to him: "Your word is good to deprive you of your fee [as a scribe], but it is not good to spoil a *Sefer Torah*." [For perhaps his intention was only to financially disturb or deprive the purchaser.] Said R. Yermiah to R. Ammi: "Granted that he has lost his fee for the Holy Names, is he to lose it for the whole *Sefer Torah*?" He replied: "Yes, because a *Sefer Torah* which lacks *Kedushat HaShem* is not worth anything."

The Rama (*Yoreh De'ah* 281:5) rules that the scribe is to receive the same compensation as that of a scribe who wrote a Pentateuch. The *Shach* (see *Nekudot HaKesef*, ibid.) notes that the fee for writing a *Sefer Torah* is much greater than the fee for writing a *Chumash*. Thus, the scribe suffers a financial loss. But, of course, some payment is made.

The *Taz*, however, notes that the Talmud clearly states that the scribe receives nothing for his services. The rationale, suggests the *Taz*, is that any *Sefer Torah* which is deemed invalid because of something not visible to the naked eye is prohibited even for private use, for such a *Sefer Torah* could easily be confused with a proper *Sefer Torah* and erroneously utilized for synagogue services.

Indeed, since an internal textual review of a *Sefer Torah* cannot disclose whether *Kedushat HaShem* permeated the process of writing it, the error of confusion is quite probable.

R. Shlomo Luria (Rashal; Commentary *Chachmat Shlomo*, *Gittin* 54b, also cited by R. Akiva Eiger, ibid., *Yoreh De'ah*) similarly questions the Talmud's statement that the scribe should receive no compensation at all for his services. According to Rabbenu Asher, the purpose of writing a *Sefer Torah* is to learn Torah therein. If so, then the purchaser still has a text for Torah study, for the fact that it lacks *Kedushat Sefer Torah* should not negate its value as a text for Torah learning, and the scribe who provided the text should be compensated. However, since such a *Sefer Torah* might mistakenly be used for public synagogue readings, R. Ammi concludes that it may not even be privately used for Torah study. It must be withdrawn from circulation and use (*genizah*).

In other words, the debate between R. Ammi and R. Yermiah is whether one can study privately with an invalid (*pasul*) *Sefer Torah*. R. Ammi is apprehensive over the possibility of invalid public use, and R. Yermiah is not concerned about such an outcome. The Halachah is according to the dictate of R. Ammi.

The position of the Rama must be that the Talmud pertains only to payment for a *Sefer Torah*. Compensation at the rate appropriate for writing a *Sefer Torah* is not granted to the scribe. However, since it is still possible to learn Torah from such a *Sefer Torah*, the minimum fee for providing a religious text should be granted. According to the Rama, there appears to be no problem with learning Torah from such a text. For this reason, some compensation is provided to the scribe.

This debate has a number of very practical ramifications.

1. Retaining an uncorrected *Sefer Torah* for more than thirty days is prohibited. It should either be corrected or put in *genizah* (i.e., buried or stored away as not fit for use) (*Yoreh De'ah* 274:1). Presumably this Halachah applies only to a *Sefer Torah* that can in fact be corrected, since otherwise the thirty-day time span would have no point. A *Sefer Torah* that lacks *Kedushat HaShem* can never be corrected. Thus, according to the *Taz* and Rashal, who both prohibit learning in such a *Sefer Torah*, perhaps there is no permission to retain it even for thirty days, for such an obstacle must be immediately removed from one's premises. On the other hand, according to Rama and the *Shach*, such a *Sefer Torah* may be retained as a text for private study.

2. Based upon Rabbenu Asher's theory that the purpose of writing a *Sefer Torah* is to use it as a text for Torah study, the Halachah is that in our day one can acquire the *mitzvah* of writing a *Sefer Torah* by obtaining religious texts (*Yoreh De'ah* 270:2).

The pertinent question is whether one may acquire the *mitzvah* in our times by obtaining a *Sefer Torah* that lacks *Kedushat HaShem*. It is apparent that neither the *Taz* nor the Rashal would consider such an acquisition valid for the *mitzvah*. The acquisition of a text that cannot be retained or utilized certainly does not meet the purpose of the *mitzvah*.

The issue relates to the position of the Rama. He contends that one may learn from such a *Sefer Torah*. Indeed, if this were not so, then the scribe who failed to manifest *Kedushat HaShem* should not receive any compensation whatsoever.

The *Shagot Aryeh* (responsum 36) notes that in the time of the *amoraim* (prior to completion of the Gemara), the prevailing practice was still to use *Sifrei Torah* as texts for study. This then may be a position of the Rama: In Talmudic times, a *Sefer Torah* lacking *Kedushat HaShem* was worthless even for Torah study. The basic reason that *Sefrei Torah* were used as texts for study was that learning Torah was still intertwined with *Kedushat Sefer Torah*. Since Torah knowledge had to be obtained from a format of *kedushah,* the *Sefer Torah* was used as the basic text. To the extent that a scribe neglected to manifest *Kedushat HaShem* (see *Gittin* 54b), the text lacked *kedushah* and was, therefore, invalid even for Torah learning. Thus, R. Ammi notes that the scribe does not deserve any compensation. The debate between R. Ammi and R. Yermiah was, possibly, whether Torah study requires *Kedushat Sefer Torah.*

After the conclusion of the Talmud, when Torah learning was expanded to include all religious texts, the firm bond of relationship between Torah and *Kedushat Sefer Torah* was no longer applicable. Thus, the *mitzvah* of writing a *Sefer Torah* was granted to all who acquired texts for Torah knowledge. A *Sefer Torah* which lacked *Kedushat HaShem* was comparable to any text used for religious knowledge. Such a *Sefer* was not categorized as an invalid *Sefer Torah* but as a religious text. It simply was not a *Sefer Torah* at all.

Indeed, the reason noted (see *Shagot Aryeh* 36, also Rabbenu Asher) for the cessation of using *Sifrei Torah* for study purposes was that it was deemed a form of belittlement (*zilzul*) of the sanctity of a *Sefer Torah* to constantly study from it. A *Sefer Torah* which lacked *Kedushat HaShem* lacked *kedushah.* Thus, there was no special sanctity that was belittled by using it as a text for study. As a result, one may also observe the *mitzvah* by the acquisition of such a *Sefer Torah.*

Another position may be that even though one may learn Torah from a *Sefer Torah* that lacks *Kedushat HaShem,* one still cannot observe the *mitzvah* of writing a *Sefer Torah* by the acquisition of such a text. Why? Perhaps the *mitzvah* is granted to texts that are not comparable in format to a *Sefer Torah.* A text that can never conceivably be interchanged with a *Sefer Torah* because of its qualitative difference is one geared solely to learning purposes. A text which merely lacks *Kedushat HaShem,* however, is obviously indistinguishable from a kosher *Sefer Torah*. If such a text could be used to observe the *mitzvah* of writing a *Sefer Torah*, the luster of *Kedushat Sefer Torah* would be diminished somewhat, because for personal, primary use there would be no distinction between a kosher *Sefer Torah* and one that lacked *Kedushat HaShem*. Perhaps, therefore, no *mitzvah* would be granted for obtaining such a text, as a means of safeguarding the sanctity of *Sifrei Torah*. The *mitzvah* may be obtained in only two ways: (1) by a kosher *Sefer Torah*, and (2) by texts which do not overtly simulate the format of a *Sefer Torah*. Thus the uniqueness of actually writing a kosher, holy *Sefer Torah* is maintained. Something that had the potential of being a kosher *Sefer Torah* but did not meet the standard is different from a text that was never comparable to a *Sefer Torah*.

The Purpose of Kedushat HaShem

A primary concern relates to the necessity for *Kedushat HaShem* altogether. Assume the following: A scribe writes a *Sefer Torah* and is fully aware that the word he is writing is one of God's Names but totally fails to manifest the process of *Kedushat HaShem*. What difference does it make whether the scribe noted that the Name was written for the sake of the *kedushah* of the Holy Name or simply as one of the numerous Names of God located in the text?

R. Yosef Rosen (*Tzafenat Pane'ach;* Rambam, part I, *Laws of Tefillin,* chap. 1, law 15) makes the following cryptic distinction. He says that the name of God has an inherent *kedushah* even when it is not in its place (see *Arachin* 6a), and therefore, when writing a *Sefer Torah* it is necessary to note that the sanctity of the Holy Name relates specifically to a *Sefer Torah*.

This concept is rooted in an understanding of the Talmudic reference cited. The Gemara reports (*Arachin* 6a) that a Gentile donated to a synagogue a beam with the Holy Name of God written on it. The Talmud suggests that the Holy Name should be carved off the beam and put aside (*Genizah*) but that the rest of the beam may definitely be utilized. The rationale offered (see Rashi) is that the Holy Name is classified as a form of

Kedushah even if it is not written in its proper syntax of words as noted in the Torah. If so, then with or without the process of *Kedushat HaShem*, the Holy Name has a degree of *kedushah*. So what additional function does *Kedushat HaShem* provide? To this the Ragashaver (R. Yosef Rosen) notes that the scribe by the process of *Kedushat HaShem* emphasizes that the Name of God is not merely an independent unit of *kedushah* but an elevated status of *kedushah* of a Holy Name intertwined within the fine fabric of Torah itself. The Holy Name is in its proper context. It is part of a sentence or Torah phrase which is interconnected with the other Holy Names and with the whole Torah. Indeed, this is the special *kedushah* of a *Sefer Torah*—the recognition that God's Holy Name is interrelated and interwoven within Torah itself. The Torah, therefore, also acquires a status of *kedushah*. Such an appreciation, of course, is not at all evident when a scribe merely recognizes the Name as one of God's Names. It is for this reason that *Kedushat HaShem* is a vital, necessary ingredient of the sanctity of a *Sefer Torah,* for it is a process that simultaneously delineates two factors: (1) that each Holy Name is in its proper place; and (2) that the words of the Torah are interrelated with Holy Names. This may be the motivation behind the *B'nai Yonah*'s rule (276) that *Kedushat HaShem* requires intention for the holiness of the Name and the holiness of a *Sefer Torah*. In other words, the Holy Name in its original setting as part of Torah is, in fact, the sanctification of the *Sefer Torah*.

An additional motivation for the process of *Kedushat HaShem* may be gleaned from *Nedarim* 7b, where Rav maintains that anyone who hears the Holy Name of God (said in vain—Rashi) and does not excommunicate the person who uttered it should himself be excommunicated. Why? Because whenever God's name is noted (in vain), poverty prevails. Tosafot and the Ran contend that this concept is derived from Scripture: "in every place where I would have My Name mentioned, I will come unto thee and I will bless thee" (Exodus 20:21). Since the mentioning of God's Name for purposes of a *mitzvah* brings blessing and wealth, mentioning it in vain is a catalyst for poverty.

The scribe, therefore, must be scrupulous in his endeavors. If for any reason even one Holy Name does not receive proper respect and intention, it is possible that instead of bringing a blessing, it may crystallize just the opposite effect. As a result, *Kedushat HaShem* is a form of safeguarding the blessings and simultaneously preventing the negative results which occur from misuse of such holy words.

Since this interpretation would cast a foreboding aura over any *Sefer Torah* that lacked *Kedushat HaShem*, it may be another reason why R. Ammi noted that such *Sifrei Torah* were totally worthless. Indeed, who would want to learn in such a *Sefer Torah*? To the extent that mention of the Holy Name for purposes of a *mitzvah* brings blessing and wealth, it is no wonder that this *mitzvah* is cherished. A *Sefer Torah* properly sanctified is the catalyst for the proliferation of blessing to all.

KEDUSHAT SEFER TORAH

Once *Kedushat Sefer Torah* is manifested prior to the commencement of the writing process, it suffices for the entire *Sefer Torah* (*Yoreh De'ah* 274:1).

R. Shlomo Ganzfried (op. cit., 4:1) quotes the *Birki Yosef*, who notes that this Halachah pertains only to the work of one scribe. However, should another scribe write something in addition to what is written by the scribe who commenced the *Sefer Torah*, he too must personally manifest *Kedushat Sefer Torah*. In other words, each scribe is required to manifest *Kedushat Sefer Torah*.

This requirement has a unique application. The common practice of scribes is to leave several letters blank upon conclusion of a *Sefer Torah*, in order to provide an opportunity for relatives and friends of the owner to be personally involved with the *mitzvah* by actually writing letters in a *Sefer Torah*. Based upon the above ruling, it is conceivable that this practice could lead to the invalidation of the entire *Sefer Torah*, if just one of these people disregarded *Kedushat Sefer Torah*. To prevent this eventuality, each person given the honor of writing a letter should overtly state that he is doing so for the purpose of *Kedushat Sefer Torah*. Another method may be for each person to be individually appointed as an agent of the scribe, so that all the writing would, in fact, be deemed a continuation of the original *Kedushat Sefer*.

Why is it necessary for the scribe to manifest *Kedushat Sefer Torah*? It should be sufficient for the scribe to note that he is prepared to write a text which will be used for the *mitzvah* of writing a *Sefer Torah*. Why the necessity of delineating that the process contains *kedushah*?

A partial response may be gleaned from the practice of making blessings before only certain types of *mitzvot*. While a *berachah* is mandated prior to the observance of such *mitzvot* as *shofar*, *lulav*, and *tefillin*, nowhere in Halachah is it required that any *mitzvah* of a social, moral nature be preceded by the chanting of a blessing. Social commandments, such as honoring parents, judging equitably, being kind to people, and giving charity, do not mandate a blessing prior to actual performance.

The distinction appears to be that only ritual *mitzvot* have blessings. Why?

An integral aspect of every blessing before a ritual *mitzvah* is the phrase *Asher kiddishanu bemitzvotav*, which literally means, "Which You have made us holy with Your *mitzvot*." The *mitzvot* are thus considered vehicles to extend *kedushah* to the Jewish people. This concept becomes apparent from a brief definition of the term *kedushah*. In Leviticus 19:2, Scripture states: *Kedoshim tihyu*—"You shall be holy"; and the Ramban notes that the *Torat Kohanim* defines this concept by the statement: *Perushim tihyu*—"You shall be separate." Thus, *kedushah* refers to that which is separate, sacred, distinct, and unique. Certain *mitzvot* definitely provide the Jew with a distinct religious dimension—a status shared only by Jews and not by others. Ritual *mitzvot* manifest such an orientation. Only Jews wear *tefillin* and blow the *shofar*. The performance of such acts visibly identifies the individual as being involved in distinctively Jewish concerns. As a result, a *berachah* is mandated. The *berachah*, formally notes that the distinctive aura of the observance is basically a form of *kedushah*. This orientation is lacking in social, moral endeavors. The ethical component is not necessarily a religious dimension but, rather, a human concern. Honoring parents and being kind are not exclusively religious observances. These acts are not distinctively Jewish in nature. As a result, performing these acts does not generate the distinctiveness of *kedushah*, and, therefore, no *berachah* is mandated (*Aruch HaShulchan, Choshen Mishpat*, 427:10).

The writing of a *Sefer Torah* is without question a visibly Jewish endeavor, qualitatively different from the writing of a book or any religious text. The form and spacing of the letters and words, coupled with the special type of parchment required, mark the process as unique and distinct.

The Jew is required to note any behavior that manifests *kedushah*. It is part of the Scriptural mandate to "be holy." At times this manifestation is through the vehicle of the *berachah*. Yet even when a *berachah* need not be chanted (see Chapter 3), the concept of *kedushah* must still be articulated. It is, perhaps, for this reason that *kedushah* must be appreciated. *Kedushah* must be noted. If not, then the distinctiveness of the *kedushah* itself is somewhat diminished.

6

Printing a *Sefer Torah*

Shortly after the invention of printing, the process was used to print Hebrew books. The first known Hebrew printed books were Rashi's commentary on the Pentateuch and, in 1475, the *Turim* of R. Yaakov ben Rabbenu Asher (the forerunner of the codes of *Shulchan Aruch*). These works as well as other classics received mass circulation amongst Jews. Printing was extolled as a holy profession which facilitated Torah learning, but a variety of questions were raised regarding the Halachic status of printed books.

In essence, the basic problem was the question of whether a printed *Sefer Torah* would have the same sanctity as one written by hand. In other words, if a printed *Sefer Torah* was equal to a handwritten one in terms of parchment, ink, form and spacing of letters and words, etc., so that the only difference was the fact that it had been printed rather than handwritten, would it have the same *kedushah* as the standard handwritten *Sefer Torah*? This Halachic problem had far-reaching practical implications, for just as the invention of printing had increased the circulation of religious texts, so too could it facilitate the proliferation of *Sifrei Torah*, reducing the cost as well as the time and difficulty of production. It could also conceivably eliminate the scribal function.

Although nowadays it is universally agreed that only handwritten *Sifrei Torah* have *kedushah* and that a printed *Sefer Torah* would be unacceptable because of its lack of sanctity, this was not always the case. Indeed, at one time there were many

Halachic authorities who regarded material produced by means of printing as equal in sanctity to material written by hand.

This orientation is exemplified by the decision of R. Binyamin Aharon b. Avraham of Solnik. A brief review of some biographical data pertaining to this sage will make it evident that he was a man of major stature and thus the ruling he issued was of great import to the community.

R. Binyamin Aharon was a Polish scholar who was considered a disciple *(talmid muvhak)* of R. Moshe Isserles (Rama) and R. Shlomo Luria (Rashal). He was a friend and peer of R. Yehoshua Falk *(the S'mah)*, R. Mordecai Yaffe *(the Levush)*, and the Maharam Lublin. After the demise of the Rama, he directed his personal Halachic problems to R. Yosef Katz of Cracow, Poland, the author of the *Sh'ayrit Yosef* (from whom I am a direct descendant). R. Binyamin Aharon was Rav of several communities and is reported to have died about 1620. His responsa entitled *Mas'at Binyamin* were posthumously published in Cracow in 1633. This volume of responsa is considered a classic work and is quoted by a multitude of subsequent venerated Halachic authorities.

The *Mas'at Binyamin* (responsum 99) was asked to rule on the sanctity of printed material.

He noted that the procedure of printing (in his day) was to form letters upon an impression which was subsequently inked and manually pressed onto parchment or paper. Letters and words formed through such a process he deemed comparable to letters and words made by placing ink on a pen and writing them. Of interest is the fact that his major concerns related to the concept of *Kedushat HaShem* (indeed, it is this issue that plays the pivotal role in deciding the status of a printed *Sefer Torah*).

In a writing system, words are formed from a pattern of individual letters grouped in a set sequence. Thus, the manual writing of a Holy Name is a sequential process whereby one letter is formed independently and other letters are added to it, one by one, to crystallize a meaningful word. In printing, however, there is no sequential process; the letters in a word are simultaneously impressed on the page. The basic question is whether this difference is a significant factor.

The *Mas'at Binyamin* ruled that it was not relevant, basing his decision on the report in the Talmud *(Yuma* 38a) about several families that had unique technical talents which they would not teach to others, among them, the family of Ben Kamtzar, which had a special writing skill that was strictly preserved within the family. The Talmud (38b) describes the skill as the ability to write with four quills simultaneously. Thus the members of this family were able to write a four-letter word with a single simultaneous action. Since they did not give the sages a (proper) response when asked why they would not teach this skill to others, the family was publicly derided by the sages. The *Mas'at Binyamin* contends that this Talmudic citation implies that a simultaneously formed word has greater sanctity than one written sequentially. The Talmud does not condemn the family for utilizing the process but for refusing to explain why it was maintained as a family secret. The implication is that the skill was an elevated process of writing. Thus, simultaneous writing of the letters of a Holy Name should definitely be an act of *kedushah*.

Perhaps, reasons the *Mas'at Binyamin*, such a simultaneous act has virtue only in relation to one word at a time. In printing, an entire column is simultaneously formed, and maybe this would make it impossible to conform to the Halachah that each Holy Name must be individually sanctified before it is written. According to Halachah, the sanctification of one Holy Name does not suffice for others. Each must be written for the sake of *kedushah*. As a result, printing of a *Sefer Torah* would not be permissible.

To this the *Mas'at Binyamin* retorts that the sanctification of each Holy Name is a requirement only when there is an interruption between Holy Names—i.e., when the scribe has to write other words between the Holy Names, another sanctification is mandated. In a case where there is no time lapse, however, and one Holy Name is written directly after another, no subsequent sanctification is necessary. The printing of a column, which forms an entire page of uninterrupted action, would be comparable to writing one Holy Name after another without interruption. Thus, printing has the same *kedushah* as writing. While the existence of this ruling suggests the possibility that there may actually have been printed *Sifrei Torah* in the *Mas'at Binyamin's* day, there are no references to such texts in the sources, and thus he may only have been stating a theoretical position.

The *Aruch HaShulchan* (1850–1908) also discusses the status of printing *(Yoreh De'ah* 271:39). Citing a number of authorities who deem printing comparable to writing, as well as an almost equally distinguished group who invalidate the printing process, he makes the following points in an effort to formulate a decisive ruling:

1. The ink used for printing may not be of the same quality as the ink used for a handwritten *Sefer Torah,* but as long as it is black, the issue is not significant.

2. The procedure of printing (in his time) was to roll paper over inked machines. As an automatic system, this is quite different from the personalized human process of writing. A *Sefer Torah* should be written by human effort, not automatically.

3. Printing lacks any intention of *kedushah.*

On this basis he concludes that printed texts do not possess the high *kedushah* of a *Sefer Torah,* but since they too are holy, albeit on a lower level, one should not burn them or treat them in a disrespectful manner.

It is evident from the *Aruch HaShulchan's* discussion that there had been many changes and technical improvements in the printing process since the time of the *Mas'at Binyamin.* The latter, in the seventeenth century, was concerned with a manual press that printed one column or page at a time, thus making it possible for the workman to have proper intentions of *kedushah* for each column. In the late nineteenth and the early twentieth centuries, printing had become an automatic process, and thus it was probably impossible to manifest specific intention for each column. Thus the views of the *Mas'at Binyamin* are not completely applicable in subsequent generations, especially nowadays, when the use of automatic printing presses, started by the pushing of a button, preclude the possibility of having independent intentions for specific portions of the work being printed. In all probability the interval between the printing of several Holy Names in different columns would be deemed an interruption between Holy Names that would warrant a specific manifestation of *Kedushat HaShem*, but since the modern printing process does not allow for specific holy manifestations, a *Sefer Torah* produced by printing would be comparable to one written without *Kedushat HaShem*. According to the *Taz* and the Rashal (op. cit.), such texts may not be used even for personal Torah study, but according to the Rama (op. cit.), one is permitted to learn Torah privately from them.

The second consideration of the *Aruch HaShulchan*—that printing is an automatic process which lacks human involvement—would be pertinent only if the writing process were part of the *mitzvah*. As has been detailed in previous chapters, the writing of a *Sefer Torah* is not an integral part of the *mitzvah*, but merely a condition necessary to prepare the *mitzvah*, and from this standpoint it should suffice if a human being pushes the button that starts the process.

Indeed, the Talmud states that "scribes of *Sifrei Torah, tefillin, mezuzot,* their agents and their agents' agent, and all who are engaged in holy work, including sellers of *techelet* [for fringes], are free from the obligation of prayer and *tefillin*" (*Sukkah* 26a). Thus all of these individuals are considered to have the same status. The writer of a *Sefer Torah* is in the same category as an agent or storekeeper who sells *tefillin*—none of them is doing an actual *mitzvah;* they are facilitators of *mitzvot,* not participants.

It should be noted that the *Mishnah Berurah* does suggest that the writing of *Sifrei Torah, tefillin,* and *mezuzot* is an integral part of these *mitzvot.*

Rashi (*Sukkah* 26a) comments on the dictum that agents of scribes are free from *mitzvot* during their endeavors. He defines their role as that of acquiring religious items from scribes in order to sell and make them available to those who need them.

The *Magen Avraham* (*Orach Chayyim* 38:8) deduces from Rashi that there is an insistence that such agents be motivated by religious concerns. If the purpose of the agent is to make a profit, then he would not be free from other *mitzvot.* The principle that involvement in one *mitzvah* frees one from another (*osek bemitzvah patur min hamitzvah*) would not be applicable. He concludes that an agent whose prime purpose is for a *mitzvah* and not to make a profit would still be freed from other *mitzvot.*

Commenting upon this ruling, the *Mishnah Berurah* (commentary *Beur Halachah,* loc. cit.) notes the following. There is a major difference between the scribes who write *Sifrei Torah, tefillin,* and *mezuzot* and their agents. The scribes are engaged in an actual *mitzvah,* but the agents are not. The placing of the *tefillin* on one's arm, for example, is the conclusion of the *mitzvah* that started during the writing process. Therefore, even if a scribe would not commence his task unless motivated by profit, once he starts, and is engaged in the performance of a *mitzvah,* there is no concern over his original desire for profit. Once he starts a *mitzvah* the assumption is that he will be solely preoccupied with the *mitzvah.* Agents of scribes however, are not performing a *mitzvah* but are merely involved in facilitating *mitzvot,* and thus they have a distinctly different role. If they truly have intentions of performing a *mitzvah* by their efforts and do not seek personal gain, then they are freed from other *mitzvot* during such involvement. If, however, their aim is simply profit, not *mitzvot,* then they are not freed from other obligations. Thus there must at least be subjective religious involvement in the *mitzvah* process.

This distinction is a forced interpretation of the Talmud, for as mentioned, all the cases appear to be lumped together as facilitators rather than performers of *mitzvot*.

Indeed, R. Naftali Tzevi Hirsch Berlin (*Meromei Sadeh, Sukkah 26a*) notes that many people have a profit or secondary motive intertwined with their performance of *mitzvot*. Is a bridegroom only concerned with a *mitzvah*? Are sellers of *tefillin* only involved in their pursuit because of *mitzvot*? Such concerns are irrelevant. The basic issue of Rashi is that there are situations wherein the scribe does not live near potential buyers. As a result, merchants provide a necessary service. If they did not provide it, the buyers would not trouble themselves to seek out the scribe. If, however, a potential buyer could easily obtain the services of a scribe, then the agent would not be essential and, therefore, would not be free from other *mitzvot*. Thus, the *Mishnah Berurah*'s ruling loses its impetus.

The *Aruch LaNer* questions the entire Halachah. The principle that frees a person from another *mitzvah* applies only when he is directly performing a prior *mitzvah*. All the above-noted cases of scribes and agents pertain to individuals who are not performing any *mitzvah* whatsoever. They are only facilitating the performance of *mitzvot*. To this he suggests that the Talmud in *Sukkah* derived the dictum from the phrase *Osek bemitzvah*. The phrase literally means "one who is involved in a *mitzvah*." Since the term is not limited to actual performance of *mitzvot*, the sages derived the rule that even necessary facilitators of *mitzvot* are free from other *mitzvot*. Thus, the scribal function is not a *mitzvah* at all. Moreover, the fact that one may purchase such items from another and still observe the *mitzvah* appears to be the basic proof that the writing process is not part of the *mitzvah*. Indeed, the Talmud labels such pursuits as "holy work," not *mitzvot*. As a result whether printing is automated or manual may be irrelevant to the issue, for writing is not a *mitzvah* at all.

The decisive concern, as noted, is that a printed *Sefer Torah* would be invalid because automatic printing provides sequential columns without any opportunity for *Kedushat HaShem*. The time factor would definitely be deemed an interruption which would require additional manifestations of *Kedushat HaShem*.

Even if one assumed that the original *Kedushat HaShem* would suffice for the entire automatic procedure, a position contrary to the mainstream of Halachah, there would still be a religious question pertaining to the writing of the letters of a Holy Name in a simultaneous rather than a sequential pattern.

Rashi (*Yuma* 38a) notes that the technical skill of simultaneously writing with four pens pertained to the writing of a *Shem* with four letters. This, of course, is translated to mean the Holy Name. The *Tosafot Yom Tov* (Mishnah *Yuma*, chap. 3) suggests that the procedure is a form of sanctification of the Unity of the Almighty, for a simultaneous action leaves no part of the Holy Name incomplete at any time, and during the normal writing process the Holy Name is not complete until concluded.

Yet the Talmud itself does not specifically state that the simultaneous writing process involved anything relating to holiness. The Talmud merely says that they could write "one word" with four pens. What that word was is not indicated. It probably did not relate to the Holy Name. In addition, the Zohar insists that the Holy Name must be formed with independent, separate letters which combine upon completion to crystallize into a Holy Name (see *Lishkat HaSofer Chakirah* 10). R. Shlomo Ganzfried rules that the Halachah is not as stated in the Zohar, but many authorities do not discard this position.

Indeed, while the writing of a *Sefer Torah* is not part of the *mitzvah*, the writing of a Holy Name may be an integral aspect of *Kedushat HaShem*. To the extent that *Kedushat HaShem* sanctifies a Holy Name in its proper format as a part of Torah, each letter needs personal attention apart from involvement with the other letters.

The *Shulchan Aruch* rules that a punctuated *Sefer Torah* is not valid (*Yoreh De'ah* 274:7). The Radbaz (*Responsa*, part 3, 643) provides the following clarification. He notes that without punctuation a variety of distinct, different meanings may be attributed to each word or combination of letters. (Mystics, in fact, derive a whole range of spiritual nuances from the association of certain letters and sounds.) A punctuated text precludes such additive spiritual considerations. Punctuation is basically an interpretation of the text. The absence of punctuation is a recognition that Torah may be interpreted in a variety of distinct variations.

The same rationale may be applicable to the printing of the Holy Name. The printing process precludes interpretations and combinations of associations of distinct, independent letters and sounds. It formalizes the Torah into words rather than letters which become words. The principle that each Holy Name must be individually sanctified suggests, perhaps, that the Holy Name, when written, should at least be in a form where an opportunity exists for distinct interpretations and intentions of a combination of letters. Thus it is indeed evident that writing, which is sequential, rather than printing, which is spontaneous, has an area of Halachic importance.

This concern serves as a possible response to a problem recently noted. The Lubavitcher Rebbe (*Hitvadut,* 2 Chanukah, 5742, *Bilti Mugah*) reports that the Holy Ari is reputed to have asked a scribe to write an entire *Sefer Torah* with the exception of the Holy Names. The Holy Ari (with unique intentions of *kedushah*) then wrote the Holy Names himself. Concludes the Rebbe: it is understood that a *Sefer Torah* written by the Holy Ari would definitely have the highest elements of propriety and *kedushah*.

Based upon this incident, the following problem is noted. *Kedushat HaShem* appears to be a major obstacle to the printing of *Sifrei Torah*. According to the experience of the Ari HaKodesh, the problem could be mitigated by printing *Sifrei Torah* without any Holy Names and then having a *sofer* personally manifest *Kedushat HaShem* by writing them by hand. This procedure, of course, would not pertain to *tefillin* and *mezuzot*, for these items are invalid if not written in their proper sequence (see *Lishkat HaSofer,* chap. 9, also chap. 20). For this reason also, perhaps, the printing of such items would not be proper, for simultaneous writing may be a violation of sequential patterns.

As a result of this question, it becomes clear that the necessity of writing a *Sefer Torah* is due, not to the effect of the written word, but to the potency of the process. There may, indeed, be no difference between the effects of writing and printing upon parchment. The concern may have been that writing by hand, because it is sequential, permits a variety of combinations and associations during the process. Any act which precludes this may lack *Kedushat Sefer Torah*. As a result, printed *Sifrei Torah* are not considered to have the same status as our traditional handwritten *Sifrei Torah*.

The concerns delineated throughout this chapter relate to the traditional Jewish respect, awe, and reverence for *kedushah*. Since printing a *Sefer Torah* may jeopardize the level of *kedushah* that our people believe a *Sefer Torah* should emanate, it is understandable why the mainstream of Halachah has tenaciously rejected any questionable text. Thus, history shows that Jews have preferred to preserve the purity of the *Mesorah* rather than seek expanded usage.

Is it any wonder? The *Sefer Torah* is a symbol of Jewish authenticity, and this concept must not be corroded by the needs of popularity. Yes, hardly anyone writes a *Sefer Torah*. But those who do preserve the *kedushah* and transmit it to the next generation.

7

Zerizim vs. *Berav Am*: Should the *Mitzvah* Be Performed Immediately?

The common practice of scribes commissioned to write *Sifrei Torah* is to intentionally leave out a number of letters (or words), or to write them in outline form, so that at a subsequent dedication ceremony, relatives and friends of the owner may be granted the honor of writing the letters in the *Sefer Torah*.

This custom poses a variety of Halachic concerns. When the last letter in a *Sefer Torah* is completed, the text (if written correctly) becomes transformed into an entity of *kedushah* and simultaneously crystallizes the fulfillment of the precept to write a *Sefer Torah*. As a result, the propriety of withholding the completion of a *Sefer Torah,* and thus postponing the observance of the *mitzvah,* until a festive ceremony at a later time appears highly questionable. Indeed, delaying a *mitzvah* is a violation of a Halachic dictum. The Talmud (*Pesachim* 4a) notes that even though a circumcision may take place according to Biblical law at any time during a boy's eighth day of life, custom requires observance in the early morning. The rationale is the general principle that the zealous hasten to perform *mitzvot* (*Zerizim makdimim lemitzvot,* hereafter referred to as *Zerizim*); i.e., the observance of *mitzvot* imposes a sense of urgency that mandates precedence over involvement in other pursuits. *Mitzvot* must not be postponed but, rather, performed at the earliest

70

available opportunity. Circumcision, therefore, should take place directly after the morning prayers. The source for this ruling is the Scriptural notation that when Abraham was told by the Almighty to bring his son Isaac as a sacrifice, he did not tarry or hesitate but arose early in the morning to commence his holy task. As it is written, "And Abraham rose up early in the morning" (Genesis 22:3—Hirsch; *Vayashkem Avraham baboker*).

Thus, the concept of *Zerizim* should obligate the scribe to conclude the *Sefer Torah* and not withhold the *mitzvah* until a later date.

It is of interest that another Halachic principle is also operative in this particular case. When choices are available one is required to select the *mitzvah* which involves the greater number of participants. This principle is derived from Proverbs 14:28, "In the multitude of people is the king's glory" (*Berav am haderat melech*; hereafter referred to as *Berav am*). It is interpreted to imply that the enhancement (*hidur*) of the Almighty is manifested by the great multitude involved in the activity. On the basis of this concept a number of practical Halachot emerge. A specific example is the ruling of the *Magen Avraham* (*Orach Chayyim* 90:9; also quoted by the *Mishnah Berurah*, ibid.) that if a person has a choice between praying at home with a *minyan* and attending a synagogue, he should attend the synagogue services. The reason is simply that the synagogue has many more worshippers and the concept of *Berav am* would prevail.

In the case at issue, both of these Halachic principles are operative. (1) If the scribe concludes the *Sefer Torah* at the earliest opportunity, he will observe the rule of *Zerizim*. (2) If he delays completion until a festive dedication ceremony, the principle of *Berav am* would be manifested. Which rule takes precedence when both cannot be observed?

Since the usual custom is for the scribe to delay final completion of the *Sefer Torah* until a dedication ceremony, the practice suggests that *Berav am* has priority over *Zerizim*. Yet a careful analysis of Halachah does not necessarily substantiate this determination.

R. Baruch Epstein (*Tosefet Berachah*, Genesis, *Parashat Lech Lecha*) notes that the Talmud (*Rosh Hashanah* 32b) overtly rules that *Zerizim* takes priority over *Berav am*. He contends, moreover, that such a decision is logical, for no one can predict the future. Obstacles of all kinds may occur. Other pursuits or events may lead to the indefinite postponement of the observance of a *mitzvah*. As a result, when a *mitzvah* becomes available, it should be immediately performed.

Close scrutiny of the Talmudic citation limits the ruling suggested. The Mishnah notes that on Rosh Hashanah the sounding of the *shofar* is appended to the *Musaf* services, while (on other holidays) the chanting of *Hallel* takes place during the *Shacharit* (morning) services. The Talmud seeks a rationale for the inclusion of these particular *mitzvot* in two distinct parts of the service.

Suggesting that the *shofar* occurs in *Musaf* because of *Berav am*, and that *Hallel* is chanted in the morning services because of *Zerizim*, the Talmud asks why *Zerizim* does not apply to the *shofar*. In other words, the principle of *Zerizim* should take priority over the rule of *Berav am*, and the *shofar* should be sounded at *Shacharit*.

To this the Talmud replies that the *shofar* is appended to *Musaf* only because of an incident that once took place. The commentaries explain that the incident occurred during a persecution of the Jews by a pagan government that forbade the sounding of the *shofar*. Since the government's agents used to frequent the synagogue only in the early morning, the *shofar* was sounded during *Musaf*, a time when no anti-Semites were present. The Yerushalmi says that at one time pagans were in the synagogue when the *shofar* was sounded. Thinking it was a stirring call for Jewish revolt, they attacked and massacred the Jews. In consequence, the sages transferred the *shofar* to *Musaf*. It was not a call to rebellion but merely another religious devotion which commenced with the *Shema*, the *Amidah*, and the reading of the Torah. If not for such traumatic historical experiences, the principle of *Zerizim* would have taken priority over the rule of *Berav am*, and the *shofar* would have been sounded during the morning service. Thus the scribe should complete his work and not wait for a dedication festivity.

It is still necessary to explain the manifestation of *Berav am* at the *Musaf* service. Why does *Berav am* have more application to *Musaf* than to *Shacharit*?

Two explanations are offered. The Radbaz (part 6, responsum 2225) suggests that in Talmudic times many people were proficient in the *Shacharit* liturgy but not in the *Musaf* liturgy, which contained Scriptural references to the sacrifices. As a result many more people came to the synagogue for *Musaf* so that the *chazzan* could include them (*motzei*) with his prayers.

The *Turei Even* (author of *Shagot Aryeh*, ibid., *Rosh Hashanah*) suggests that people came late to services. Thus, the later the *shofar* was sounded in the services, the more people were present to hear it. Having more people in the synagogue at *Musaf* was the manifestation of *Berav am*.

As a result, the Talmud in *Rosh Hashanah* may not be used as a general precept that *Zerizim* has priority over *Berav am*. The Talmud relates to a situation where a large number of worshippers are present at both *Shacharit* and *Musaf*, but the number present at *Musaf* is greater. In such a case *Zerizim* (*Shacharit*) represents a public synagogue, which is a form of *Berav am*. However, where the choice is between observing the *mitzvah* privately (such as by the scribe concluding the *Sefer Torah*) and observing the *mitzvah* publicly in the midst of a synagogue festivity, perhaps the concept of *Berav am* takes precedence. As a result, no proof may be cited from the Talmud in *Rosh Hashanah*. Indeed, this may be one reason why the scribal custom has prevailed.

R. Baruch Epstein (op. cit.) notes the Halachic preference to have a *minyan* in attendance at a circumcision. He contends that the source for this custom is the Biblical verse which states, "On the selfsame day [*be'etzem hayom*] were Abraham and Ishmael his son circumcised" (Genesis 17:26, Hirsch). The commentaries note that this implies that the circumcision occurred at the strength of the day; namely, at noon or during the time of the sun's greatest heat. The reason, suggests R. Epstein, was that at such a time circumcision was a public affair. The problem, however, is that this would imply that Abraham himself, when faced with a choice between *Zerizim* and *Berav am*, selected the latter. From this case, R. Epstein notes, no generalization may be made, for (as previously noted) the Talmud (*Rosh Hashanah* 32) has decided that *Zerizim* takes priority. Abraham's case was unique. Since circumcision, especially at Abraham's advanced age, was an extraordinary event, the public act in the afternoon was necessary as a way of manifesting his pride and lack of fear from any mortal source. Abraham's public circumcision was an act of defiance against the world. Abraham was a believer and wished the world to know it. As a result, he needed the concept of *Berav am*. Others, however, must follow the rule that *Zerizim* takes precedence.

Yet based upon the theory that *Zerizim* is granted priority only when it manifests some public nature in itself, it is possible that the incident of Abraham's circumcision is in reality substantiation for the view that *Berav am* takes precedence over *Zerizim* when the latter is truly a private concern.

Why should the concept of *Berav am* be significant in the determination of a *mitzvah*? What difference does it make whether the *mitzvah* has a few or a thousand participants?

One answer may be that numbers enhance the beautification of a *mitzvah* and thus are a form of *hidur mitzvah*. Just as one is obliged to seek out a beautiful *talit* or *tefillin*, so too should one be involved with many others in the performance of *mitzvot*. Beautifying a *mitzvah* manifests a high degree of appreciation. So too with numbers. The more people involved in a *mitzvah*, the greater the manifestation of respect and appreciation. If this is the rationale for *Berav am*, then it should be noted that the *Magen Avraham* (*Orach Chayyim* 25:1) rules that a *mitzvah* should not be delayed even if it may be subsequently performed in a more qualitative, beautiful fashion (see *Mishnah Berurah*, ibid.). In other words, the concept of *Zerizim* takes priority over *hidur mitzvah* (the beautification of a *mitzvah*). Thus, the scribe should immediately conclude the *Sefer Torah* and not await any ceremony.

Yet this ruling is not totally applicable to the concept of *Berav am*. It is suggested that the motivation for the concept of *Berav am* is not necessarily the beautification of a *mitzvah* but, rather, its status as a public *mitzvah* (*mitzvah derabbim*). The involvement of multitudes in a *mitzvah* transforms the act into something comparable to a public *mitzvah*, which has priority over a private *mitzvah*. A *mitzvah* that lacks *Berav am* is categorized as a private *mitzvah* in comparison. Thus, *Zerizim* has application to the timing of the performance of a private *mitzvah*. When a *mitzvah* can be performed either at an early date or later on, *Zerizim* mandates the earliest possible performance. Public *mitzvot*, however, are in a category by themselves, for they do not depend upon personal schedules.

The writing of a *Sefer Torah* relates to a variety of public *mitzvot*. It simulates the aura of Sinai. It is used for *Keri'at HaTorah*. By withholding completion until a public ceremony may take place, the scribe is emphasizing the public status of the *mitzvah*, a status that would not be manifested if the *Sefer Torah* were privately concluded. Indeed, when the subsequent performance of a *mitzvah* not only displays *Berav Am* but may also be a true public *mitzvah* that requires a *minyan*, then it is logical to assume that one must await such an action.

Some corroboration of this concept may be provided by the following. The Talmud (*Ketubbot* 8a) discusses the specific *berachot* chanted at a wedding. Rashi notes that the blessing *Shehakol bara lichvodo*—"That everything was created for His glory (honor)"—is basically a *berachah* commemorating the assemblage of guests, which brings glory to the Almighty. As a result, it should properly be chanted whenever there is a gathering of people. Why is it placed at the beginning of the blessings for a bride and bridegroom (under the *chuppah*), directly after the *berachah* for wine? Rashi suggests that the reason is that the Talmudic sages generally group several *berachot* together whenever the blessing for wine is intoned (e.g., *Havdalah*—wine, spices, light). As a result, this *berachah* was made part of the seven general *berachot* for a bride and bridegroom.

What was Rashi's original conception of the proper moment

to chant the *berachah* of *Shehakol bara lichvodo*? Logic would presume Rashi's position to be that the *berachah* should have been chanted before the ceremony whenever a crowd had assembled. To the extent that some definition of an "assemblage" is necessary, perhaps the *berachah* should have occurred whenever more than ten Jews assembled. Thus, Rashi would be of the belief that the concept of *Zerizim* takes precedence over the principle of *Berav am*, which certainly will be manifested by the large number of people observing the *chuppah*. In other words, the concept of *Zerizim* would have mandated the *berachah* prior to the *chuppah*. It is chanted later on together with other blessings only because of the tendency to group *berachot* adjacent to a blessing for wine.

This case is comparable to the citation in *Rosh Hashanah*. While a crowd is present at the beginning of a wedding, a larger number is present at the *chuppah*. It is for this reason that *Zerizim* takes precedence over *Berav am*. Yet when the concept of *Zerizim* pertains to a wholly private *mitzvah*, there may be no priority over a subsequent *mitzvah* performed *berav am*.

The Tosefet Rid (ibid.) suggests an alternative motivation for the *berachah* of *Shehakol bara lichvodo* being part of the blessings for a bride and bridegroom. He notes that the priority of this *berachah* (after the blessing for wine) is that blessings under a *chuppah* require a *minyan* and there is *berav am*. The meaning may be as follows. The *chuppah berachot* requires a *minyan* and, therefore, manifest the status of a public *mitzvah*. In such a circumstance, *Berav am* is not overshadowed by *Zerizim*. This definitely suggests that a public *mitzvah* which also contains *Berav am* is granted preference.

So too with the writing of a *Sefer Torah*. The *Sefer Torah* is so closely intertwined with *kedushah* and public *mitzvot* that its completion should properly manifest its public nature. As a result, scribes should be encouraged to continue their historical practice. Again it is to be noted that Jewish customs are rooted in Halachic concerns and not mere devices for gala public parties.

8

The Last Letters of a *Sefer Torah*

The owner who commissions a scribe to write a *Sefer Torah* is generally provided with an opportunity to personally write (or fill in) several letters or words in the *Sefer Torah*. It is of interest to determine whether there is any Halachic mandate regarding this matter. Namely, is the scribe or the owner free to select any words or letters he wishes, or are there specific Halachic suggestions? The usual practice is for the scribe to leave the last letter unwritten and to exercise his personal preference regarding additional words. Though not generally known, there does seem to be a Talmudic source indicating a Halachic concern that certain specific items should be personally written by the owner.

The Talmud (*Bava Batra* 14a) states: "The rabbis reported to R. Hamnuna [the tradition] that R. Ammi wrote four hundred *Sifrei Torah*. Said R. Hamnuna to them, 'Perhaps he only wrote [the Scriptural verse] *Torah tzivah lanu Mosheh* ["The Torah which Moshe commanded us is an inheritance of the congregation of Jacob"; Deuteronomy 33:4].' " Rashi contends that the tradition of R. Ammi's writing four hundred *Sifrei Torah* does not refer to actual *Sifrei Torah*, for no one has the time to engage in such a tedious endeavor. Rather, it relates to the writing of one verse (*Torah tzivah lanu*) four hundred times. Rabbenu Tam (ibid.) notes that this verse is called (or equated with) Torah. His substantiation is the citation in *Sukkah* 42a, where the Talmud remarks that "when a child is able to speak [i.e., reaches the maturational level at which talking is possible], his father teaches him Torah. What is Torah? Said R. Hamnuna, [the verse] *Torah tzivah lanu Mosheh.*" Thus, the term *Sifrei Torah* is not to be taken literally. The Maharsha (ibid.) adds to the theory of Rabbenu Tam by suggesting that R. Ammi wrote the verse four hundred times (as texts) for children.*

The *Shitah Mekubbetzet* brings a number of authorities who relate R. Ammi's activity to the actual writing of *Sifrei Torah*.

1. According to the Ri ibn Migash, whosoever writes the verse *Torah tzivah lanu* is considered as if he wrote the entire Torah.
2. According to Rabbenu Asher, R. Ammi commissioned scribes to write four hundred *Sifrei Torah*, directing them to inform him when they came to the verse *Torah tzivah lanu* because he wished to write it by himself since it is called Torah, as cited in *Sukkah* 42a.
3. According to the Ra'avid, the case of four hundred *Sifrei Torah* is based upon the Talmud in *Menachot* 30a, which states: "A person who acquires a *Sefer Torah* is considered as if he grabbed a *mitzvah* from the street; one who writes a *Sefer Torah* is considered as if he accepted it from Mount Sinai. *Should he write one verse or correct one letter*, it is considered as if he wrote [the *Sefer Torah*]." Note the phrase "Should he write one verse." This phrase is not found in the standard editions of the Talmud. The position of the Ra'avid must be that the correction of one letter is deemed important only when the *Sefer Torah* has an error and requires correction. Thus, the writing of a letter in a kosher *Sefer Torah* has no specific Halachic function. One is granted the status of having personally written an entire *Sefer Torah* only if one actually writes an entire verse. Since the verse *Torah tzivah lanu* is categorized as comparable to the entire Torah (*Sukkah* 42a), it should be written by the owner himself.

*The Yerushalmi, *Sukkah* 17b, says that a child who is learning to talk should be taught *Lashon HaTorah*. The *Korban Edah* states that this is a requirement to teach a child Hebrew.

The commentary of the Ritva (*Bava Batra* 14a) quotes the *Yad Rama*, who deduces from this Talmudic citation (*Bava Batra* 14a) that whoever writes the verse of *Torah tzivah lanu* in a *Sefer Torah* for the purpose of a *Sefer Torah* is deemed as if he wrote the entire *Sefer Torah*. If not, then what function would be served by writing this verse? The Ritva takes note of the Ra'avid's position but contends that R. Hamnuna's dictum does not relate only to a situation where one purchases the *Sefer Torah*, for it is unlikely that R. Ammi actually bought four hundred *Sifrei Torah*. Thus, even in a *Sefer Torah* which belongs to another (if one cannot afford to buy a *Sefer Torah*), the entire *mitzvah* of writing a *Sefer Torah* may be observed by writing the verse *Torah tzivah lanu Moshe*.

On the basis of the preceding discussion, the scribe should be instructed to leave blank space in the *Sefer Torah* for the verse *Torah tzivah lanu*, and the owner himself should either write or fill in its letters. By this process the owner is deemed as if he himself had actually written the entire *Sefer Torah*. What owner who commissioned a scribe to write a *Sefer Torah* would not wish to gain this additional Halachic benefit?

Another aspect for consideration is the writing of the first letter or word of the *Sefer Torah*. The Talmud (*Horayot* 12b) states that the practical method of observing the *mitzvah* of *Vekidashto* ("And you shall make him [the *kohen*] holy"; Leviticus 21:8) is by granting the *kohen* the opportunity to be first in all matters pertaining to *kedushah*. The *kohen*, therefore, is the first to make the blessings over the Torah. Thus, being first has a special elevated status, especially in matters pertaining to *kedushah*. The Rosh Yeshivah of Rabbenu Chaim Berlin (HaGaon HaRav Yitzchak Hutner, *z.l.*) once noted that anything done in the world may be equaled or surpassed by another except the quality of being first. That status is unique. No one can replicate its role. It stands alone. For this reason, perhaps, the owner should be granted the opportunity to personally write or fill in the first letter or word in the *Sefer Torah*. Thus, he alone has the distinction of having started the *Sefer Torah*. This process moreover, crystallizes yet another obligation. The Talmud contends that whoever starts a *mitzvah* (*hamatchil bemitzvah*) should conclude it, for the status of the *mitzvah* is granted to the one who concludes the *mitzvah* (*Sotah* 13b). Thus, if A started a *mitzvah* and B concluded it, B is considered as if he had performed the *mitzvah*. The owner, therefore, should also write the last letter of the *Sefer Torah*. He should be the one who actually concludes the *Sefer Torah*. Indeed, he and no one else should be granted the privilege of writing the one letter which upon its completion transforms the written text into a *Sefer Torah* of *kedushah*.

At the dedication ceremony, it is customary to grant a number of individuals the honor of writing letters in the *Sefer Torah*. What is the Halachic status of this practice? What Halachic function or *mitzvah* is performed by writing a letter in a *Sefer Torah*?

The Talmud (*Menachot* 30a) and the Rambam (*Hilchot Sefer Torah*, chap. 7, law 1) rule that whoever corrects even one letter in a *Sefer Torah* is considered as if he had written an entire *Sefer Torah*. The circumstance by which the writing of but one letter is tantamount to the writing of an entire *Sefer Torah* requires explanation. Assume that a *Sefer Torah* has several errors and someone corrects only one of them. Since the *Sefer Torah* is still not kosher, it would be illogical for the person who corrected one letter to be entitled to the status of having written an entire *Sefer Torah*. A *Sefer Torah* with eight errors is no more usable than one with seven errors. The Biblical *mitzvah* is the finished product, and someone who writes four-fifths of a *Sefer Torah* does not acquire four-fifths of the *mitzvah*. Until the *Sefer Torah* is concluded, no *mitzvah* whatsoever is fulfilled. The ruling of the Rambam is, as the *Kiryat Sefer* notes, that writing one letter is considered the same as writing an entire *Sefer Torah* only when such "correction makes the *Sefer Torah* complete and kosher." The Rama (*Yoreh De'ah* 270) explicitly so rules. On the basis of this preliminary analysis, the writing of any letter (except the last) would not be granted the status of fulfilling the *mitzvah*.

In addition, the *mitzvah* is conferred only upon those who have ownership of the *Sefer Torah*. A guest who is given the honor of writing a letter has no ownership rights in the *Sefer Torah*. He is merely serving in the role of a scribe. Just as a scribe commissioned to write a *Sefer Torah* does not observe the *mitzvah* at all and is but a facilitator of a *mitzvah* engaged in holy work, so too, the honored guest is granted the privilege of being involved with holy work. The honor of writing a letter in a *Sefer Torah* may be in the same category as kissing the *tzitzit*; a means of expressing love for the *mitzvah* (*chibuv mitzvah*).

If, however, the guest is granted ownership of the letter, then the status of the entire *Sefer Torah* is altered. The *Sefer Torah* is no longer the exclusive possession of one Jew but becomes a joint venture of partners. Would someone who paid for a *Sefer Torah* wish to share that *mitzvah* with someone who writes but one letter? In addition, there are Halachic authorities who question whether a jointly owned *Sefer Torah* fulfills the *mitzvah*. Their position is that each Jew must personally and exclusively own his own *Sefer Torah*. In other words, transferring the ownership of even one letter would jeopardize the status of the original owner.

There is another interesting consideration that may alter the status of the previous analysis. R. Shlomo Kluger (*Tuv Ta'am VeDa'at*, part 1, responsum 232) was asked to rule upon the following problem: A man commissioned a scribe to write a *Sefer Torah*. In the middle of the writing process, the owner died. The heirs decided to continue the *Sefer Torah* and on its completion paid the scribe for his services. Who has the *mitzvah*, the father or the children?

R. Kluger reports that R. Ephraim Margolit (*Beit Ephraim, Yoreh De'ah*, responsum 63) discusses a comparable issue in a case of partners who both wrote part of a *Sefer Torah*. R. Margolit rules that each partner should have a status no less than that of someone who corrects a letter in a *Sefer Torah* (in other words, both should be granted the *mitzvah*). R. Kluger disagrees, contending that only the person who actually completes the *mitzvah* should be graced with the *mitzvah*. The father in the question posed above and the partner who wrote part of the *Sefer Torah* but did not conclude it are not granted the *mitzvah* at all. As it is written in *Sotah* 13b, "A *mitzvah* is granted to the person who concludes it."

An initial reaction is that logic supports the position of R. Margolit. In the case where one letter was corrected and the *Sefer Torah* is still unfit for use, everyone would agree that the correcting of the one letter has no Halachic significance. Since the *Sefer Torah* is not kosher, the correction did not alter the status of the *Sefer Torah*. However, where someone wrote only one letter and others subsequently corrected or completed the entire *Sefer Torah*, the one letter plays a most vital role. If not for that letter, the *Sefer Torah* would not be kosher. As a result, upon completion of the *Sefer Torah*, any and all who wrote letters (with, of course, rights of ownership) should be confirmed as having performed the *mitzvah* of writing a *Sefer Torah*. Thus, at a dedication ceremony those who are granted the privilege of writing letters (as well as the ownership of such letters) should, upon completion of the *Sefer Torah*, be granted the status of the *mitzvah*.

Indeed, it is difficult to understand R. Shlomo Kluger's rationale, which would totally disregard the role of anyone but the person who completes the mitzvah.

The following tentative distinction, based on the fact that there are different types of partnerships, is suggested:

1. In one kind of partnership, each partner exclusively owns a distinct segment of a whole. As this relates to a *Sefer Torah*, Partner A totally owns one half, and Partner B owns the second half. Partner B has no ownership rights in Partner A's segment, and vice versa. In such a situation, R. Kluger's position may have validity. Since Partner A has no share, ownership, or control over the conclusion of the *Sefer Torah*, he is not granted the *mitzvah*. His role is comparable to that of someone who writes one letter and leaves the *Sefer Torah* unfit for use. In such a case, even if someone else eventually concluded the *Sefer Torah*, and the correcting of one letter made it easier for him to accomplish the completion process, the writer of the one letter would still not be granted the

mitzvah, because the *mitzvah* is only granted to an effort which is directly related to the completion process. Partner A has no control or influence over Partner B, so only Partner B receives the *mitzvah*, because he is the one who completed the *mitzvah*. Had he withheld his efforts, the activity of Partner A would have been meaningless.

2. There is another form of a partnership in which there is no exclusivity of ownership. As it pertains to a *Sefer Torah*, both partners jointly own each letter and word. Partner A writes the first part and Partner B concludes the *Sefer Torah*, but each letter is a joint venture. As a result, it would not matter who actually writes the last letter, because he is merely the agent of the other partner. The last letter, which completes the *Sefer Torah*, is jointly owned, controlled and shared by the partners. In such a venture, perhaps even R. Shlomo Kluger would agree with R. Ephraim Margolit, that both receive the *mitzvah*.

Thus, at a dedication ceremony, the writers of letters, if granted ownership, become partners in the *mitzvah*. If ownership is limited to the letter written, then according to R. Kluger, the action is devoid of a *mitzvah*. If partnership in the entire process is granted, then the writing of but one letter is graced with the status of writing an entire *Sefer Torah*.

It should be noted that the owner should reserve at least the last letter for himself. If he grants ownership in the letters to the guests, then by giving away the honor of the last letter he may be jeopardizing his entire *mitzvah*. Also, it is a great *zechut* (privilege) for him to complete such a great *mitzvah* with his own hand.

In a situation where ownership is not granted, consideration should be given to the Ritva's position that the writing of the verse *Torah tzivah lanu mosheh* conveys the *mitzvah* to the writer even without ownership. This honor may be granted to a distinguished guest without jeopardizing the owner's *mitzvah*. The overwhelming majority of Jews cannot afford to observe the *mitzvah* of actually writing a *Sefer Torah* or commissioning a scribe to write one. What a *zechut!* What a privilege it is to be granted the opportunity to write the *Torah tzivah lanu* verse. The Ritva's position is truly another mechanism to enable those without funds to observe the Biblical *mitzvah.*

While many scribes are unaware of this consideration, logic suggests that the ancient custom should be reactivated. Indeed, it may even be that the entire *Torah tzivah lanu* verse need not be written. Perhaps the first and last letters of the verse would suffice.

It should again be emphasized that the writing of a letter in a *Sefer Torah,* in any role other than as an agent of the scribe, requires a specific manifestation of *Kedushat Sefer Torah.* As a result, each person graced with the honor of writing a letter should vocally state that he is writing it for the purpose of *Kedushat Sefer Torah.* If this phrase is not invoked, the *kedushah* of the *Sefer Torah* may be impaired. The *Kedushat Sefer Torah* chanted by the scribe at the commencement of the *Sefer Torah* relates only to his personal efforts and not to the work of others (see Chapter 5; also, *Keset HaSofer* 4:1).

Thus, ceremonial festivities relate to the integrity of the *Sefer Torah* itself. The preceding analysis is but an attempt to highlight a variety of such vital concerns.

THE FIRST LETTER OF THE TORAH

It was noted that in matters pertaining to *kedushah,* the quality of being first is a significant status. As a result, "The owner should be granted the opportunity to personally write or fill in the first letter or word in a *Sefer Torah.*" A young *rosh hayeshivah* has astutely commented that this suggestion only applies prior to any writing by the scribe. Once the scribe has written the second letter or word of a *Sefer Torah,* any subsequent writing by the owner would no longer be categorized as first.

Though the comment has validity pertaining to the status of being first, there is additional motivation for the owner to write the first (and last) letter. The Talmud states, " *U-re'etem oto, uze-chartem, et kol mitzvot HaShem*—You may look upon it, and remember all the commandments of God' [Hirsch, Numbers 15:39]. This *mitzvah (tzitzit)* is comparable to all the *mitzvot*" (*Menachot* 43b). Rashi (ibid.) says that the word *tzitzit* has the numerical value of 600; there are eight strings and five knots (on each corner of a garment) which comprise the number 613 (see also *Tosafot, Menachot* 39a and *Tur, Shulchan Aruch, Orach Chayyim* 24). Thus, by looking at the *tzitzit* one may be reminded of the 613 commandments.

The custom of the *Mahari Berunah* was to hold only the *tzitzit* on the corner adjacent to his heart during *Keri'at Shema*; count five knots and eight strings, and together with the value of the word *tzitzit* (which is 600) recall the 613 commandments. Also, since the word *tzitzit* is singular, and Scripture states "*U-re'etem oto*—You may see *it*," a singular term, only one of the four corners was used (Responsum 100).

Common practice, however, is to gather the *tzitzit* on all four corners and hold them together during the *Shema*. Even though by use of the singular form Scripture indicates only one corner, the *minhag* may symbolize that all four corners unite to represent one *mitzvah*. Yet this custom does not reflect the relationship to the 613 commandments previously noted.

The *Tashbatz* (268) presents an alternative theory by noting that there are eight strings on each of the four corners, which together comprise thirty-two *tzitzit*. The number thirty-two is significant in that it is the same numerical value as the first and last letters of the Torah. The first letter is a *bait (BeReishit)*, which has the value of two, while the last letter is a *lamed (Yisrael)*, which has the value of thirty. So, by observing the thirty-two *tzitzit*, one recalls the beginning and end of the Torah, which have the same numerical composition. Thus, an activity which serves as a catalyst for the remembrance of the 613 commandments is meritorious.

If so, then perhaps the owner of a new *Sefer Torah* should be encouraged to personally write these two letters to dramatically indicate the totality of Torah and *mitzvot*.

9

The Scribal Function and the *Mitzvah* to Learn Torah

The scribal function is classified as a form of "heavenly work" (*melechet shamayim; Sukkah* 26a). When writing a *Sefer Torah* in his professional capacity, the scribe facilitates the observance of a *mitzvah* for someone else. As a result, the scribe's professional role assumes a religious aura. Of particular interest are the personal Halachic ramifications for the scribe while engaging in the process of writing a *Sefer Torah*.

The *Shulchan Aruch* (*Orach Chayyim* 47:3) rules that "one who writes *divrei Torah*, even though he does not read [them aloud], is required to chant the *Birchat HaTorah*." Thus, writing Torah is considered a form of learning Torah; otherwise *Birchat HaTorah* would not have been mandated for the process. This suggests that the personal *mitzvah* of learning Torah each day may be fulfilled by writing a *Sefer Torah*. Based upon this Halachah, one could contend that a scribe who writes a *Sefer Torah* for someone else is simultaneously acquiring the benefit of observing his personal *mitzvah* to learn Torah. This may, therefore, be a more finely honed definition of the "heavenly pursuit" of the scribe; namely, that it is a process whereby one who helps another to acquire a *Sefer Torah* is himself granted the *mitzvah* of learning Torah.

Yet it is difficult to generalize from this Halachah because several critical comments severely limit its pragmatic application.

1. The *Taz* (ibid.) contends that the Halachah applies only to a scribe who has intentions to learn (Torah). However, one whose purpose is to make a profit (and not to learn) is not required to chant the *Birchat HaTorah*; for writing a Torah solely for profit is not considered Torah but is comparable to writing a letter which contains some Torah within it. (The implication of the *Taz* is that such a letter does not require a *Birchat HaTorah* because the Torah it contains was not included for Torah learning purposes.)
2. The *Magen Avraham* (ibid.) notes that the above Halachah is restricted to a person who is writing texts for himself in a learning process and comprehends what he writes. A scribe, however, who merely copies Torah and does not seek comprehension, is not required to chant the *Birchat HaTorah*, for such a process is not considered learning (Torah).
3. The *Shulchan Aruch* further rules (ibid., 47:4) that *hameharer*, someone who merely thinks Torah thoughts but does not orally vocalize the Torah studied, is not required to chant the *Birchat HaTorah*.

Both the *Taz* and the *Magen Avraham* contend that this Halachah clearly contradicts the ruling that the process of writing *Torah* mandates a *berachah*. They argue that there is a general principle that where speech or oral statements are required, the process of writing is not comparable to or equated with speech. Writing Torah, therefore, is not on the same level as orally learning Torah. As a result, if the process of thinking and understanding Torah does not mandate a *berachah*, then writing Torah should be in the same category and also not mandate a *berachah*.

Based upon the above comments, the *Shulchan Aruch HaRav* (47:3) rules that writing Torah without oral vocalization does not require a *berachah* because it is comparable to *hirhur*, an internal thought process. A scribe who does not actually learn Torah may chant the *Birchat HaTorah* for his scribal function only if he orally vocalizes some of the Torah he is writing. In other words, pragmatic Halachah does not rely upon the ruling of the

Shulchan Aruch that requires *Birchat HaTorah* for only writing Torah.

The *Mishnah Berurah* (ibid.), in his commentary *Be'ur Halachah*, suggests that the position of the *Taz*—namely, that a scribe who writes Torah for the profit motive is not categorized as learning Torah—may relate only to a process which lacks oral Torah. In other words, the *Taz* takes the position that writing Torah only for profit does not require a *berachah*, but if the scribe orally intones Torah, then perhaps, even if the purpose is for profit, such efforts are categorized as Torah which mandates a *berachah*. The *Be'ur Halachah* does not rule on this case and pragmatically notes that the scribe should each day impose upon himself the obligation to actually learn some verses of the Torah subsequent to the chanting of the *Birchat HaTorah*.

The equation of writing Torah with the process of thinking Torah requires analysis. There is a simple logical distinction between these two facets of learning Torah. The writing of Torah is a manifestation of an action; the thinking of Torah lacks such action *(ma'aseh)*. In general a *berachah* is chanted prior to the performance of the action of a *mitzvah*. As a result, the action of writing Torah requires a *berachah*, but thinking about Torah, because it is an internal process, does not require a *berachah* (see *Levush*, ibid.). It is necessary to ascertain why this distinction is not accepted by Halachic authorities.

Indeed, the above rationale may serve as a response to the incisive remarks of the Vilna Gaon, who pointedly questions the ruling that "thinking Torah" does not require a *berachah*. The Vilna Gaon notes that the basic Scriptural mandate to learn Torah is the verse *Vehagita bahem*—"And you shall dwell [in the words of Torah]" (Joshua 1:8). This means that the purpose of learning Torah is to be involved in comprehension, which is an internal process.

Indeed, is not intense thought a key ingredient in the acquisition of knowledge? Torah learning is not an empty ritual to be studied by rote, devoid of comprehension. Meaning is essential to the learning process. As a result, the position of the Vilna Gaon appears to be most creditable. A person whose mind is involved in analyzing and thinking Torah issues certainly appears to be on a higher level of Torah than one who merely reads one verse orally! As a result, the process of thinking Torah should require a *berachah*.

The previously noted distinction surely applies to this problem. Thinking Torah may certainly be a form (even a lofty form) of learning Torah. The lack of a *berachah* for thinking Torah thoughts does not imply that such a process is not a means of observing the *mitzvah* of learning Torah. *Berachot* were instituted only prior to actions, and since the process of thinking Torah thoughts is a purely internal function which lacks an overt action, no *berachah* was ordained. Thus, the lack of a *berachah* does not diminish its luster. However, since the final Halachic authorities contend that even the writing of Torah should not require a *berachah*, it is necessary to analyze why thinking Torah should also not require a *berachah*.

It is apparent from the preceding discussion that there is a three-way debate concerning the requirement of *Birchat Ha-Torah*.

1. The *Shulchan Aruch* mandates a *berachah* for both writing Torah and reading Torah out loud.
2. The *Magen Avraham, Taz, Shulchan Aruch HaRav,* and *Mishnah Berurah* mandate a *berachah* only for reading Torah out loud.
3. The Vilna Gaon insists that a *berachah* should be chanted even for just thinking Torah thoughts.

A possible explanation may be as follows: The Talmud (*Temurah* 14b) states that originally both the oral reciting of the written Torah (Pentateuch; see Tosafot) and the writing of the oral Torah were prohibited. This suggests that the method of studying the Pentateuch was once limited to an oral reading process. Chanting sections of the Torah by heart was a violation of this rule. Torah had to be read aloud. Silent reading or reading by sight without audibly pronouncing the letters and sounds was also not considered valid. Why? Torah also had another stipulation. It had to be a form of speech, which is vocal. As it is written, "And you shall talk of them" *(vedibarta bam)* and "To speak of them" *(ledaber bam)*, verses which apply to Torah (see Deuteronomy 6:7, also Deuteronomy 11:19). Thus, Torah was an oral reading process resembling speech. Any aspect of Torah learning that lacked this component of speech was not part of the original *mitzvah* to learn Torah. Yet speech or oral language alone was not sufficient. Written Torah had to be read, not expounded orally. In addition, it is possible that the distinction between reading and thinking was that reading was a vocal process and anything not vocal was not considered speech.

In *Berachot* 11b a hypothesis is presented that *Birchat HaTorah* is to be chanted only for the study of Scripture and not for the study of Mishnah and Talmud. No one, of course, would even conjecture that the study of Mishnah and Talmud was not considered Torah. The position was that a *berachah* requires the subsequent action of a *mitzvah*. The written Torah had to be studied only through the action of reading. Oral Torah had no such requirement; for it is based upon comprehension and meaning and not a ritual reading process. In addition, a *berachah* generally requires the utilization of some ritual object. The written Torah was embodied in the *Sefer Torah,* which is an object of *kedushah.* Oral Torah had no textual body (for writing it was prohibited) and no requirement of a specific action (such as reading). As a result, it was contemplated that only the Pentateuch required a blessing. Later on, when writing the oral Torah was permitted, the Mishnah and the Talmud assumed some aspects of the original decree: namely, that Torah, regardless of whether it was written or oral, had for purposes of *Birchat HaTorah* to manifest the vocal reading element. In this fashion, the historical similarity to the original method of learning Torah prevailed. Thus, thinking Torah thoughts does not mandate *Birchat HaTorah.* Also, since writing is not equal to speech, no *berachah* is chanted.

The position of the Vilna Gaon may be that once *Birchat HaTorah* was extended to oral Torah, the requirement for an object of a *mitzvah* or a specific action was discarded. The *berachah* now relates to the process of learning and comprehension regardless of format. As a result, even thinking Torah requires a *berachah*.

The *Shulchan Aruch* may contend that the extension of *Birchat HaTorah* to include the oral Torah did not preclude the requirement of a specific action. Yet such action need not be restricted to speech or reading. As a result, the action of writing Torah requires a *berachah*.

Another possible theory is that the position of the *Shulchan Aruch* relates to an analysis of why reading Torah aloud was required. It may be suggesting that audible Torah is qualitatively different from silent Torah. The *Shulchan Aruch* may be pinpointing an essential element of Torah education itself.

Torah is not just a form of knowledge. It is an interlocking religious bridge connecting us to the past, lived in the present, and directed to the future. It is *Mesorah,* a way of life transmitted from past to present, from generation to generation, with the understanding that it will be given to our children to create further links to the future.

Perhaps this is the true meaning of the Halachah that requires a *berachah* only for vocal or written Torah; for only through such a process can Torah be transmitted to another generation. Torah that is solely within the mind may be vastly creative, analytic, and brilliant, but it remains within the individual. No one can hear such thoughts. Torah learning should emulate the tradition of Sinai. In *Pirkei Avot* it says, "Moshe accepted the Torah from Sinai and transmitted it to Joshua, and Joshua to the elders, and they [gave it] to the prophets, who transmitted it to the men of the Great Assembly." In other words, Torah is a gift that must be granted to others. It is not proper to obtain knowledge and then jealously guard it solely for one's own personal gratification. Torah has a dual responsibility. It must be learned and it must be taught. Vocal Torah may be overheard, and written Torah may be studied by someone else.

A *berachah* for Torah learning is required only when the process emulates the tradition of Sinai. Only Torah that intertwines *Mesorah* into its core is the type of Torah that merits a *berachah*. This theory is derived from the decision of the *Aruch HaShulchan* (*Orach Chayyim* 47:10) that writing Torah requires *Birchat HaTorah* because the writing process is a means of teaching and preserving Torah. Thus, the *Birchat HaTorah* refers not to action or objects of *kedushah* but to the process of transmitting it to another generation.

It is suggested, moreover, that the three-way debate mentioned above does not relate to the *mitzvah* of learning Torah but only to the requirement of chanting the *berachot*. As a result, a scribe, even one who is commissioned to write a *Sefer Torah*, may himself observe the *mitzvah* of learning Torah. Several observations are still necessary.

1. The scribe, whatever his primary motivation, should at least be interested in learning—i.e., he should utilize the copying of a *Sefer Torah* as means of reviewing his own Torah knowledge. While the scribal function as such may not be a learning process, the scribe should manifest an orientation toward learning.

2. It may be questionable as to whether comprehension is absolutely necessary for the process of Torah learning. The *Birchat HaTorah* are not necessarily blessings for the actual learning of Torah. Indeed, the conclusion of the *berachah* is the phrase *La'askok bedivrei Torah*—"To be involved with the words of Torah." This suggests a dual aspect of Torah. A person may learn Torah, which implies meaning and comprehension, or may merely be involved with Torah, which is not necessarily a learning process. The *b'rachah* is for the involvement with Torah. Thus, someone who desires to learn (attempts to learn), even if he lacks the ability to comprehend what he learns, may at least observe the facet of being involved with Torah.

3. The fact that the scribe is fundamentally engaged in his efforts because of the profit motive should not detract from the essence of his Torah, as long as he also exhibits an intention to learn Torah (see Chapter 6). Indeed, the scribe should be in the same status as a teacher of Torah. No one

questions the latter's *mitzvah* of learning Torah even though he would relinquish his position if his remuneration were stopped. The desire for profit thus does not detract from the *mitzvah* if the intention is to perform the *mitzvah*.

There is still another unique factor relating to the study of Torah that the scribe performs. The Mishnah (*Sotah* 20a) rules that a *sotah* (a woman who was accused of committing adultery by her husband and in fact was found to have done so) was able to postpone her punishment by producing evidence of *zechut*, i.e., of having performed some meritorious deed. In a discussion of the type of deed that could postpone punishment, the following concepts are articulated in the Talmud (*Sotah* 21a): If the deed was the act of learning Torah, women who learn Torah are in the category of those who are not commanded yet (voluntarily) observe (see Rashi—their reward is not comparable to that of those who were commanded), and thus it does not have sufficient standing to suspend punishment. If the deed was the performance of *mitzvot*, (tradition has it that) *mitzvot* provide protection from troubles only when being performed, not afterward. Torah (however) provides protection even after the learning concludes. Thus, *mitzvot* do not have the capacity to withhold punishment. Ravina notes that the *sotah* did, indeed, have the merit of Torah. Her involvement with Torah was not her personal Torah learning but the toil and effort of bringing her children to learn Torah and of waiting for her husband, who would go to another city in order to learn Torah.

Based upon this Talmudic citation, HaRav Hutner, *z.l.* (*Pachad Yitzchak, Shevu'ot, ma'amar* 13) derives the concept that bringing children to learn Torah (or waiting for a husband who is learning Torah) must be an act that is granted a reward comparable to the actual learning of Torah itself. For the Talmud specifically notes that only deeds of Torah and not of *mitzvot* can suspend punishment. To the extent that the process of bringing children to Torah is deemed to contain sufficient merit to withhold punishment, it must be because it is equal to learning Torah itself.

HaRav Hutner, *z.l.*, further suggests that this principle

equating the reward of the facilitator to the reward of one who learns Torah is an exclusive precept limited to Torah and not pertaining to the performance of *mitzvot*. For example, a person who enables another to observe the *mitzvah* of honoring his parents is not granted the reward of long life which is granted those who honor their parents. The rationale is that Torah has a unique status. The Talmud contends (*Menachot* 99b; see Rashi) that when Torah learning is halted for such *mitzvot* as a wedding or a funeral, a reward is granted as if one had continued to learn Torah. The reason is that the commitment to perform *mitzvot* is a necessary condition of the *mitzvah* to learn and is an observance of the ultimate goal of Torah itself (*lilmod al minat la'asot*). Now, if the reward of Torah is given to one who ceases learning in order to perform *mitzvot*, should it not be granted to one who facilitates Torah learning?

It has been noted that Rabbenu Asher rules that the writing of a *Sefer Torah* is for the purpose of learning Torah. Thus the scribal function is the facilitation of Torah learning. Based upon the position of HaRav Hutner, z.l., the scribe should be granted the same reward that would be granted for actually learning Torah. As a result, even if the Halachah holds that the scribal function of writing a *Sefer Torah* is not categorized as actually learning Torah, it acquires the reward of such a process. Thus the scribal profession is most assuredly a "heavenly pursuit."

10

Pronouncing the Holy Names While Writing a *Sefer Torah*

The relationship of the scribal function to the scribe's personal *mitzvah* of learning Torah has yet another unique Halachic consideration.

The writing of a *Sefer Torah* requires a manifestation of *Kedushat HaShem*. Thus, before writing each Holy Name of the Almighty, the scribe must express his intention of writing it solely for the purpose of sanctifying the Holy Name (see Chapter 5). A Halachic concern relates to the propriety of the scribe's accurately pronouncing the Holy Names during the process of writing a *Sefer Torah*.

During *Tefillah*, *Keri'at HaTorah*, and the observance of *berachot*, the chanting of the accepted, accurate pronunciation of the Holy Name is mandated. On other occasions, the prevailing custom is to substitute the word *HaShem* for any occurrence of the Name of God. (The denotation of the Hebrew word *HaShem* is "The Name"; its connotation is that it refers to "The Holy Name of the Almighty.")

This custom is a pragmatic Halachic device to sustain and preserve the integrity of the Holy Name. Indeed, the Rambam contends that a practical application of the Biblical mandate "To fear God" (Deuteronomy 10:20) is to refrain from utilizing His Holy Name in vain, for nonpurposeful usage would reflect a lack of proper awe (and consideration) (see *Sefer HaMitzvot*, *mitzvah* 4). Thus, it is clear why a substitute term was developed.

Of interest is the proper procedure for the pronunciation of the Name of God during the process of learning Torah. Does a person who is studying the Pentateuch or even the Talmud have the right to accurately pronounce a Holy Name appearing in his text, or must he substitute the term *HaShem*?

Personal observation of popular usage notes that those who are learning Torah texts generally use the word *HaShem*. Yet certain Halachic authorities provide definitive rules that differ from the accepted custom.

The *Taz (Orach Chayyim* 621:2) contends that the accurate pronunciation of God's name, similar to the pronunciation during *Tefillah,* is permitted when one is reading an entire verse of Scripture. He further notes that when a substitute term is utilized, it should be the word *HaShem* rather than the word *Adoshem* (a term used by the masses). The *Kitzur Sh'la,* moreover, reports (*Mesechet Shevu'ot,* p. 196) that even though it is a sin to mention God's name in vain, it is a *mitzvah* to pronounce it correctly while learning Torah and not to use the substitute word *Adoshem.**

An analysis of the rationale for the Halachic positions regarding proper use of the Holy Name during Torah learning may suggest guidelines for the scribe who writes a *Sefer Torah.*

The position of the *Kitzur Sh'la* may be that the proper pronunciation of the Holy Name is restricted to the performance of *mitzvot.* Indeed, the proper sounding of a Holy Name is the signal that a *mitzvah* is being observed. For example, if the word *HaShem* were utilized during the *Keri'at HaTorah,* it would immediately be recognized as an error that had to be rectified. Since learning Torah is certainly a *mitzvah,* one should acknowledge its status by correctly pronouncing each Holy Name. Thus, according to the authorities who contend that the scribal function is a form of learning Torah, the scribe not only should

---

*The preference of the *Taz* for the term *HaShem* may have a twofold basis: (1) *HaShem* is an authentic Hebrew word, while *Adoshem* combines the correct initial sound of God's name with the word *shem* ("name"); (2) *HaShem* is used in the prayers of Yom Kippur.

be permitted but also should be encouraged to accurately pronounce God's Name. Indeed, associating God's Name with learning Torah may be a lofty method of expressing awe for the Divine Name. It certainly is not a mark of disrespect.

The position of the *Taz* may be that since learning Torah is a *mitzvah*, it is wrong to prohibit anyone from utilizing the proper pronunciation. Yet no guideline of preferential usage should be granted. Why? Perhaps because mandatory usage is restricted to acts that are specifically required by Halachah. Learning Torah is a *mitzvah*, but the choice of the particular text used for this purpose is left to the individual's own discretion. Since there is no requirement to observe the *mitzvah* by studying a text that contains a Holy Name, the correct sounding is not mandated. This consideration would also apply to a scribe. However, someone who personally writes his own *Sefer Torah* in order to observe the Biblical *mitzvah* may be required to pronounce the Holy Name to manifest the obligatory nature of the *mitzvah* process.

The writing of a *Sefer Torah* should not have a status different from that of *Keri'at HaTorah*. In both cases, a *mitzvah* is being performed, and it is mandatory to complete certain specific passages of the Torah that include a Holy Name. Yet there is still a distinction, for the scribe is not obligated to utilize his scribal function as a means of learning Torah, especially for verses that contain a Holy Name. As a result, no preferential pronunciation should be mandated.

There is another and more compelling motivation for the *Kitzur Sh'la*'s position. The Talmud (*Berachot* 6a) notes that the Holy One, Blessed be He, is present in a synagogue and anywhere that ten people pray (even if not in a formal synagogue), as well as in a three-member court of Jewish law and when two persons are studying the Torah together. The Talmud then says, "And how do you know that even if one man sits and studies the Torah the Divine Presence is with him? For it is said: 'In every place where I cause My Name to be mentioned, I will come unto thee and bless thee' [Exodus 20:21]." On the phrase "I will cause My Name to be mentioned," Rashi says,

"When My Name will be mentioned for My *mitzvot* and My words." Rashi thus suggests that God's Name may be properly sounded during words of Torah. R. Epstein (*Tosefet Berachah*, Exodus, *Parashat Yitro*) specifically states the rule that whoever learns Torah and comes across the Name of God should pronounce it correctly and not use the substitute term *HaShem*. The reason is that the Talmud specifically states that the verse presents evidence to substantiate the presence of the Holy One when only one person learns Torah. The issue must be that pronouncing God's Name is the catalyst for His Divine Presence. The Presence requires the sounding of God's Name, not a substitute term.

Note also the Maharsha, who clearly says that the Talmud refers to pronouncing God's Name during the learning of Torah. In other situations, sounding the Name would be an example of nonpurposeful usage of the Holy Name (ibid.).

Indeed, it may be demonstrated that in Talmudic times the general custom was to accurately pronounce the Holy Name while learning Torah.

The Mishnah (*Berachot* 13a) rules that "if one was reading in the Torah [the section of the *Shema*] when the time for its recitation arrived, if he has *intention*, he has performed his obligation." The Gemara notes that if such intention refers to a concern to observe the *mitzvah* of chanting the *Shema*, then this Mishnah may be used as a source to substantiate the view that *mitzvot* must be performed with specific intent. If such intent is lacking, the Mishnah rules, the *mitzvah* of the *Shema* is not observed. The Gemara concludes that the Mishnah relates not to an intention to perform the *mitzvah* of the *Shema* but, rather, to reading the *Shema* accurately. Tosafot (ibid., 13a) clarifies the issue by noting that the case relates to a person checking the Torah for spelling errors. Such a person does not read the text in a proper fashion. Should he, moreover, have the intention of accurately reading the Torah text with its proper pronunciation, then he may also observe the *mitzvah* of the *Shema*.

Now, if Holy Names were not to be accurately sounded during the process of learning Torah, then even if this person was reading the Torah, and not just reviewing spelling errors, he still would not be graced with the *mitzvah* of the *Shema* for his efforts. The *Shema* includes a variety of Holy Names; and one certainly could not observe the *mitzvah* by utilizing the term *HaShem*. Therefore, since the Talmud rules that anyone who actually reads the Torah portion of the *Shema* is ipso facto granted the *mitzvah* of the *Shema*, it overtly suggests that Torah learning of Holy Names manifests the proper pronunciation of such Names.

An additional Talmudic citation which appears to corroborate this concept is the rule (*Berachot* 22a) that a *ba'al keri* (one who has had a seminal issue) may "expound the Talmud, provided that he does not mention the Divine Names that occur" (in the Biblical verses so expounded; see Rashi). This definitely suggests that the Holy Names were properly pronounced during the learning process, for if the term *HaShem* had been utilized, there would have been no reason to exempt a *ba'al keri*.

On the basis of this principle, it may be suggested that anyone who fails to pronounce God's Name correctly and instead utilizes the word *HaShem* withholds the Divine Presence from his learning of Torah. Who would wish to be in this category? Indeed, this would make the correct sounding of God's name not just a preferred usage but a mandatory act.

As this theory relates to the scribe, moreover, a most vital consideration is manifested. The scribe is mandated to express *Kedushat HaShem* before writing each Holy Name. What greater expression of concern for the sanctity of each Holy Name could there be than an attempt to utilize the Holy Name as a means of crystallizing the Presence of the Almighty in the writing of a *Sefer Torah*? As a result, perhaps scribes should be instructed to use the scribal function as a learning process and to orally vocalize each Holy Name as it is written.

Yet, as previously mentioned, the usual custom is to utilize the term *HaShem* during the learning process. The basis for this may be the decision of the *Magen Avraham* (*Orach Chayyim* 215:5) that an adult who is studying the *berachot* noted in the Talmud should not accurately pronounce the Holy Name while doing so. This rule is also recorded by the *Shulchan Aruch HaRav* (*Orach Chayyim* 215:2). The *Aruch HaShulchan* similarly so rules and adds the Halachah that those who present public Torah lectures should chant the term *HaShem* when reciting verses that contain a Holy Name. He notes that there are authorities who disagree, but concludes that it is proper to refrain from such a leniency and that such is the custom. The *Mishnah Berurah* (*Orach Chayyim* 215:13) reports the ruling of the *Magen Avraham* but notes that one may sound the Name accurately if one is reading Scriptural verses in the Talmud. The latter rule is based on the decision of the Yavetz, who reports that it was the custom of his father, the Chacham Tzevi (see *Sha'arei Teshuvah, Orach Chayyim* 215).

Thus, the consensus of Halachic authorities is that the Torah process of studying a *berachah* does not entail permission to properly sound the Holy Name. However, this rule is not to be extended to the process of learning Scriptural verses. In the latter case, no substitute term for the Holy Names is mandated (see ibid. and *Mishnah Berurah,* loc. cit.). Thus, it is necessary to clarify the distinction between these cases.

The *Shulchan Aruch* (*Orach Chayyim* 215:3) rules that it is "permitted to teach children the [proper] sequence of *berachot,* even though they are making a *berachah* in vain during the learning process." This implies that permission to properly pronounce the Holy Name is granted only to children, for purposes of *chinnuch,* but not to adults for purposes of Torah study. It does not contradict the Talmudic citations previously noted that appear to encourage the proper sounding of Holy Names during study of Scriptural verses.

The Torah was originally transcribed in written form to be a text for study—as it is written: "and teach it to the children of Israel (Deuteronomy 31:19). Every word in the Torah, including all the Holy Names, was originally designed for purposes of Torah study. As a result, during Torah study the accurate pronunciation of the Holy Names is permitted, because that is their normal, anticipated utilization. Indeed, that is why the Talmud regarded the learning process as an activity graced by the Presence of the Almighty. Nonetheless, certain limitations prevail. The *Taz* (*Orach Chayyim* 621:2) rules that proper pronunciation of a Holy Name is permitted only if one reads an entire verse. As an integral part of the syntax of a Biblical verse, a Holy Name has to be read in its proper context. There is a general principle that "any verse wherein Moshe Rabbenu did not stop, we are not permitted to stop," (*Megillah* 22a). Thus, in *Keri'at HaTorah* a break in Torah reading occurs only at the conclusion of a verse. As a result, the Holy Name is properly read only upon completion of an entire verse. Any other procedure would be a deviation from its normal format.

In addition, the Holy Name is part of a text which was originally only to be read, not orally invoked (*Temurah* 14b). For this reason, perhaps, the *Aruch HaShulchan* is correct in maintaining that during a lecture one should use a substitute term for each Holy Name. Again, any deviation from the original format mandates use of the term *HaShem*.

This may also be the reason why the proper sounding of the Holy Names is not permitted while studying *berachot*. The Talmud (*Berachot* 40b) notes that the essence of a *berachah* is the inclusion of a Holy Name. The Name, therefore, is not a tool for study but is to be used only when a *berachah* is required. During Torah study, the Holy Name is utilized in a process which deviates from its original format. For this reason the term *HaShem* must be chanted.

The practice of also using the word *HaShem* during the Torah learning of Scriptural verses, as a means of preserving the integrity of the Holy Name, may possibly, therefore, be a misguided stringency. Proper utilization of the Names may instill a greater degree of respect in the learning process and also serve as a catalyst of the Holy Presence. As it pertains to a scribe who is required to manifest both *Kedushat HaShem* and *Kedushat Sefer Torah*, the analysis given above suggests a marked preference for the proper pronunciation of Holy Names.

The *Shulchan Aruch* (*Yoreh De'ah* 274:2) and the Rama (*Orach Chayyim* 691:2) rule that a scribe should orally vocalize each word prior to writing a *Sefer Torah*. The Beit Yosef (*Yoreh De'ah*, loc. cit.) says that this is a means of safeguarding against error. In addition, it simulates the original *Sefer Torah*, of which the

Talmud says: *Moshe omer vekotev*—"Moshe Rabbenu orally stated and then wrote" (*Bava Batra* 15a). The *Bach* (*Orach Chayyim* 32) theorizes that the holy sanctity of the Biblical words vocalized (somehow) has an impact upon the writing process.

Each of the three reasons suggests a different orientation to the pronouncing of the Holy Names.

1. If vocalization is a means of attaining accuracy, then the scribe should pronounce the words as they are written and not as they are sounded. (Also, maybe he should pronounce the letters, not the words.) The Holy Name cannot be pronounced as written and therefore, perhaps, should not be pronounced at all (see *Sh'not Chayyim, Sefer S'tam* 86, quoted by *Lishkat HaSofer* 5:6).

2. The *Beit Yosef* cites the *Mordechai*, who derives from the Talmud (*Bava Batra* 15a) the notion that Moshe Rabbenu did not vocalize the last eight verses of the Pentateuch, which relate to his death. Thus, if tragic events need not be pronounced, it is certain that the vocalization of a Holy Name, which may be a sin, should also not be pronounced (*Lishkat HaSofer*, loc. cit.) (See *Aruch HaShulchan, Yoreh De'ah* 274:7, who concludes that Moshe's nonutterance of the last eight verses proves that the scribe's failure to verbalize does not invalidate a Sefer Torah.) In addition, Moshe Rabbenu utilized the true, accurate pronunciation of each Holy Name. We, today, do not have such knowledge. Since we cannot imitate Moshe, perhaps no vocalization of a Holy Name is necessary.

3. According to the *Bach*, vocalization of each Holy Name should be required as a means of conveying sanctity to the written word.

   Then what is the scribe to do? According to the previous analysis that it is permissible and proper to vocalize God's Name during a Torah learning process, each scribe should be instructed to utilize his scribal function as a means of learning Torah; thus, he may be permitted to properly pronounce God's Name.

11

Reading the Torah at the Consecration of a New *Sefer Torah*

At the consecration services for a new *Sefer Torah,* the custom *(minhag)* is to open the new *Sefer Torah* and publicly read therein the concluding fifteen verses, commencing from *Meonah Elokai kedem* (Deuteronomy 33:27) until the end. It is of interest to probe the rationale for this *minhag,* as well as the reason for selecting these specific verses.

R. Malkiel Zevi Halevi (Rav of Lomza) offers the following explanation.

The Talmud states that as Moshe Rabbenu wrote the first *Sefer Torah* his process was *omer vekotev,* "to verbalize [each word] and then to write [it]" (*Bava Batra* 15a). Thus, the scribe emulates Moshe Rabbenu (the original scribe) by verbalizing each word written in a *Sefer Torah.* Yet the Talmud specifically deletes any reference to vocalization for the last eight verses of the Bible, which relate to Moshe's death. It states: *kotev be-dema*—"written with tears" (ibid.; see commentary *Anaf Yosef* [*Ayn Yaakov*], who analyzes the Vilna Gaon's position that *dema* means a "mixture"; a form wherein all letters converge without space for the endings of words or sentences). As a result, the scribe who replicates Moshe need not verbalize the last verses.

At a ceremony for a new *Sefer Torah,* there may be an intention to manifest not only that the entire Pentateuch was recently written but also that it was studied. Indeed, the scribe vocalized each word as he wrote it, yet this Torah learning was not complete, for the last eight verses were never chanted. Thus it is necessary to publicly read the Torah in order to conclude the learning process. To the extent that custom is not to commence *Keri'at HaTorah* with tragic events (such as the death of Moshe), [see *Megillah* 31b], the reading starts with a verse proclaiming the glory of God and Israel (Deuteronomy 33:27).

While logic would suggest that the scribe himself should serve as the reader to proclaim his personal conclusion of the study of the Pentateuch, the common custom is not for the scribe to serve as the *ba'al koreh*. Perhaps, suggests R. Malkiel Zevi Halevi, the scribe has intention to listen to the Torah reading and to privately vocalize the verses heard (*Divrei Malkiel*, part I, responsum 3:10).

This theory implies that Moshe Rabbenu's process of first verbalizing and then writing the Torah was, indeed, a directive that the scribal function was to always be an integral facet of Torah learning. The scribe of a *Sefer Torah* is not to be a mere copyist. The Torah is to be written through the process of Torah learning, and each scribe must verbalize words to emphasize the Torah-learning factor inherent in the scribal process.

The major difficulty with this theory is that common practice does not require the scribe who wrote the *Sefer Torah* to be in attendance at the dedication services. According to the above rationale, his presence is vital to the ceremony. The fact, moreover, that the *ba'al koreh* is not the scribe mitigates against any theory which interrelates the scribal *mitzvah* of completing a segment of the Torah and the ceremony itself.

Though the ceremony may not relate to the scribe's personal involvement with concluding the study of the Pentateuch, it may refer to the fact that the Pentateuch itself has been completed. That is, the combination of the scribe's learning and the public reading of the concluding verses (which the scribe did not vocalize) marks a significant event. It manifests the fact that as a result of a *Sefer Torah* having been written, the Pentateuch was completely studied. This adds a unique dimension to the dedication of a new *Sefer Torah*, for some authorities contend that the completion of any of the twenty-four books of the Bible constitutes an act which creates a raison d'etre for a *Seudat Mitzvah* (see *Penai Yehoshua, Berachot* 17a, also *Minchat Pitim,* and *Da'at Torah, Orach Chayyim* 55). Thus, the public reading of the Torah is the process whereby the learning of the Pentateuch is officially completed. The ceremony becomes comparable to the completion of a tractate of the Talmud. Dedicating a *Sefer Torah* and reading therein publicly creates an aura whereby all are directly involved in the pursuit of Torah learning, the goal of the *mitzvah.*

The entire theory, is based on the principle that the scribe's vocalization of Biblical words is synonymous with Torah learning. This, of course, may not be the case (see Chapter 9).

The *minhag* to publicly read the final verses of the Bible may be derived from another source. The Talmud states (*Bava Batra* 15a) that the last eight verses of the Bible are to be read by a *yachid* (i.e., one person). Rashi interprets this to mean that the verses should be read in their entirety (without interruption). There are numerous other interpretations for this citation (see, for example, Rambam, *Hilchot Tefillah,* chap. 13, law 6; Mordechai, *Chacham Zevi,* responsum 13). The *Shittah Mekubbetzet* presents two novel interpretations. They are:

1. Whoever reads (in the Torah) a few verses prior to the last eight verses which describe Moshe's death is not permitted to read until the conclusion, for this would intermingle words written by Moshe with words written by Yehoshua. Such a person must conclude directly before the last eight verses, and another person should be called solely to read the latter portion. This procedure formally delineates the last portion as distinct, for it was written by Yehoshua, not Moshe.
2. Whoever reads the Torah verses prior to the last eight verses is *not* permitted to cease his reading at the last eight verses. No one should be called solely to read the latter portion, for the part that Moshe wrote and the latter verses should be joined together, so that there is no noticeable distinction

between what was written by Moshe and what was written by Yehoshua (*Shittah Mekubbetzet, Ri Ibn Migash, Bava Batra* 15a).

Based upon the latter interpretation, the selection of the last fifteen verses to be read at the dedication service for a new *Sefer Torah* is to publicly emphasize that all parts of the Torah are equal to each other in sanctity. This is *Torat Moshe,* and no section is more important than any other.

12

Adding or Deleting a Letter in a *Sefer Torah*

The writing of a Sefer Torah requires care and attention to ensure accuracy. Should but one letter be missing or one extra letter be added, the text will not be graced with *Kedushat Sefer Torah* (Rambam, *Hilchot Sefer Torah*, chap. 7, law 11; see also chap. 10, law 1, rules 12 and 13). This concern for accuracy is reflected in the following Aggadic tale (*Eruvin* 13a):

> When R. Meir became a student of R. Yishmael, the latter asked him, "My son, what is your profession?" R. Meir replied, "I am a scribe." To this R. Yishmael remarked, "My son, be scrupulous in your profession, for it is a heavenly pursuit, [and] should you delete one letter or add one letter, such effort [is tantamount] to destroying the entire world."

The omission or addition of a single letter not only withholds *Kedushat Sefer Torah* but also represents a reprehensible activity which is classified as comparable to destroying the world. Such a harsh status is indicative of a severe religious error, but the simple addition or omission of a single letter does not overtly appear to warrant such a negative reaction. Early rabbinic authorities, therefore, present specific examples to demonstrate how a scribal error of but one letter can transform Holy Writ into an expression of non-Jewish theological beliefs.

The problem, as Rashi notes, is exemplified by the way the

meaning of the phrase "God is truth" would be totally per-
verted if the first letter of the Hebrew word for "truth" (*emet*)
were omitted, changing it to "death" (*met*). To cite another
example, the phrase "And God spoke" appears frequently in
Scripture. The addition of one letter, a *vav*, to the verb "spoke"
would make it a plural, thus providing grounds for a denial of
monotheism. Tosafot points out that the addition of one letter
to the verb "created" in the first verse of the Book of Genesis,
making it a plural construct, would pose the same danger.
Moreover, as the Maharsha (ibid.) indicates, according to the
mystical tradition all the letters of the Torah taken together
comprise the Name of the Holy One, and thus the deletion of a
single letter would be a form of diminishing the Holy Name.
The *Midrash Rabbah* (Leviticus 19 and Song of Songs 5) cites a
variety of Scriptural verses wherein the miswriting of one letter
may lead to theological deviations. Such errors are described as
comparable to "destroying the world." Thus, Rashi and Tosafot
have precedent in relating scribal errors to theological distortions.

Indeed, this may be the reason why the *mitzvah* of learning
Torah was originally intertwined with the concept of *Kedushat
Sefer Torah*. A *Sefer Torah* is a text whose accuracy has been
verified. Thus there are assurances that the student will not be
misled by the text. A *Sefer* that lacks *Kedushat Sefer Torah* may
contain textual distortions that could lead students astray. As a
result, such a text should not be utilized even for private study.
Perhaps, therefore, to ensure the purity and accuracy of Torah
study, only a kosher *Sefer Torah* was utilized.

The preceding discussion clarifies why certain specific errors
of even one letter are destructive and merit condemnation. It is
still necessary to explain why errors that do not alter the
meaning of a text should also be classified as "destructive of the
world."

For this reason, R. Shlomo Ganzfried's position (*Lishkat
HaSofer* 1:1) seems to manifest a more general application.
R. Ganzfried maintains that a scribe who deletes or adds a letter
is regarded as causing others to sin. This is because everyone

who assumed the validity of the *Sefer Torah* with the missing or added letter and chanted the *Birchat HaTorah* over it would be taking God's Name in vain. In addition, the scribe would be creating the false impression that the *mitzvah* of writing a *Sefer Torah* had been observed when, in fact, it was not. Thus, instead of facilitating *mitzvot*, in accordance with his proper role, the scribe would be facilitating religious error and sin.

It is of interest to determine whether the very act of omitting or adding a letter in a *Sefer Torah*, even if it does not alter the meaning of the text, is regarded as a sin in itself, regardless of the consequences to others.

Scribal errors of this kind should be regarded as overt violations of the Biblical injunction against adding to or diminishing from *mitzvot*, for Scripture specifically states, "Thou mayest not add thereto [*lo tosef*] nor diminish from it [*lo tigra*]" (Deuteronomy 13:1; Hirsch translation). These prohibitions, moreover, are included in the 613 primary Biblical *mitzvot* (see Rambam, *Sefer HaMitzvot*, prohibitions 313, 314; also *Sefer HaChinnuch*, *mitzvot* 454, 455).

Rashi, in his commentary on the Pentateuch (Deuteronomy 4:2), delineates the following definitions: "*Lo tosefu*: five *parshiyot* in *tefillin*; five species [inclusive] of *lulav*; and five strings of *tzitzit* [each, of course, regularly has only four]. And so [is the case with] *Lo tigru*." By implication, three *parshiyot* in *tefillin*, three species on Sukkot, and three strings of *tzitzit* would be violations of *Lo tigru*.

Thus, a scribe who adds an extra letter to the *Sefer Torah* or who omits even one letter would be in direct violation of the Biblical mandate. What difference is there between adding a string to *tzitzit* and adding a letter to a *Sefer Torah*?

It may, however, be demonstrated that there are a number of distinctions between the two cases.

The Talmud (*Rosh Hashanah* 28b) states:

> How do I know that a *kohen* who goes up to *duchan* [the platform whereupon the *kohanim* stood] should not say, "Since the Torah granted me permission to bless [*Kelal*] *Yisrael*, I will add a *berachah* of my own; for example, 'May God, the God of your fathers, add to

you a thousand times as many as ye are now' [Deuteronomy 1:1; Hirsch]?" [Because such action is prohibited by the verse] Lo tosefu ["You mayest not add"; Deuteronomy 4:2].

The *Sefat Emet* (ibid.) remarks that one should not infer from this citation that a *kohen* is prohibited from greeting other people with the blessing of *shalom*. Such an action would certainly not be within the purview of the Biblical injunction. Why? Because the Talmud specifically disallows only the adding of extra blessings to the act of performing the *mitzvah* of *Birchat Kohanim*. Indeed, the Talmud relates to a *kohen* who "went up to the *duchan*" to bless the people. The implication is that the Biblical injunction applies to an extra *berachah* appended to the regular *berachot* during the actual observance of the *mitzvah*. Thus, a kohen may extend personal blessings to friends throughout the day without qualms about violating Biblical *mitzvot*.

This theory appears to be essential to an understanding of the practical application of *Lo tosef*. If someone made *tefillin* with five *parshiyot* and/or *tzitzit* with five strands but did not put on the *tefillin* or wear the *tzitzit*, he would not be violating the Biblical law. The violation occurs only during the performance of the *mitzvah* and not during its process of preparation. The scribe does not perform the *mitzvah* of writing a *Sefer Torah*. He is merely a technician who prepares a text with which others observe the *mitzvah* (see the discussion in Chapters 3 and 6). As a result, scribal errors should not be classified as violations of the Biblical injunctions of *Lo tosef* and *Lo tigra*. A scribe who makes an error is in the same category as someone who placed five strings in a garment and never wore it.

However, a scribe who writes a *Sefer Torah* for himself, or an owner who completes a *Sefer Torah* and adds or omits a letter, is in a distinctly different category. Yet it may be suggested that even such persons may not be in violation of the Biblical laws. The *Turei Even* (author of the *Shagot Aryeh*) notes Rashi's observation (loc. cit.) that violating the prohibition of *Lo tigra* involves an action that is the diametrical opposite of the action entailed in violating *Lo tosef*. For example, adding a fifth string to the four *tzitzit* would be a violation of *Lo tosef*, and using only three strings would violate *Lo tigra*. To this theory, the *Turei Even* presents the following counterargument.

The simple definition of the term *Lo tigra* is a prohibition against diminishing a *mitzvah*. This suggests that a *mitzvah* is, in fact, being observed but is somewhat lacking in its full complement of requirements. The sole case mentioned in the Talmud as an example of *Lo tigra* manifests this principle. In a situation where the omission of a facet of the *mitzvah* invalidates the *mitzvah* itself, *Lo tigra* is not violated. Thus, the utilization of three strings in *tzitzit* is not an example of diminishing a *mitzvah*, because three strings in *tzitzit* is not a *mitzvah* at all.

To substantiate this theory, the following Talmudic case is cited (*Sukkah* 31a–b): "[One must have] four species [inclusive] of the *lulav*. Just as one may not diminish [its number], so too may one not add [to them]. Should one not have an *etrog*, one cannot bring . . . a pomegranate or any other matter" (31a). On the latter phrase, the Talmud (31b) poses the question that such a ruling is self-evident and did need to be stated. To this the Talmud replies that such a rule is quite necessary, for in the event that *etrogim* were not available, one might assume that it was permitted to use a comparable fruit, so as not to forget the concept of an *etrog* and to sustain memory of the need for four species. To counter such an assumption, the rule was recorded, for the use of a fruit other than an *etrog* might create confusion concerning proper observance in an era when *etrogim* were available.

Thus, the *Turei Even* logically reasons, the Talmud negates the use of a fruit other than an *etrog* solely to forestall possible confusion or to prevent future problems. If not for this concern, there would be no reason to prohibit the use of a pomegranate instead of an *etrog*. Yet on Sukkot one must have four specific species. Substituting a pomegranate for an *etrog* would not, in reality, be a Halachic replacement for the *etrog*. It would be deemed as if one were attempting to observe the *mitzvah* with three required species, rather than four, and this would not be an observance of the *mitzvah* of having four species on Sukkot. Now, if *Lo tigra* is applicable even when the *mitzvah* is not observed at all, then the Talmud should have prohibited the use of a pomegranate because of the Biblical injunction of *Lo tigra*. This prohibition, of course, has no relationship to problems over future observance. To the extent that the Talmudic citation does not refer to any Biblical prohibition, it must be because *Lo tigra* is not violated when a *mitzvah* is not observed (see the glosses of R. Akiva Eiger, *Sukkah* 31a, who cites the *Turei Even* on this matter).

Thus, notes the *Turei Even*, in cases where the absence of a vital requirement invalidates the *mitzvah*, *Lo tigra* is not applicable even if one has intentions of observing a *mitzvah* (see *Sefer Avnei Miluim*, appended to *Sefer Turei Even, Rosh HaShanah* 28).

On the basis of this theory, the scribal omission of a letter would not be a violation of *Lo tigra*, for such a text would lack *Kedushat Sefer Torah* and the *mitzvah* of writing a *Sefer Torah* would not be observed.

The *Turei Even*'s theory may also relate to *Lo tosef*. Perhaps one violates *Lo tosef* only when one observes the requirements of the *mitzvah* and adds on to them. In a situation where the basic rules of the *mitzvah* are not observed, it may be that *Lo tosef* is also not violated. Thus the addition of a letter to a *Sefer Torah* would not be an infringement of *Lo tosef*, for *Kedushat Sefer Torah* requires an accurate number of letters. Any additional letter invalidates the *Sefer Torah*. Once the extra letter is written prior to the conclusion of the text, *Kedushat Sefer Torah* never transpires. Thus, when the Torah is finished, *Lo tosef* would not be applicable.

Yet even according to this line of reasoning, *Lo tosef* may still occur if the scribe adds a letter after accurately completing the *Sefer Torah*. This would be a classic example of adding to the requirements of a *mitzvah* once it has been observed properly.

A response to this observation may relate to the essence of the *mitzvah* of writing a *Sefer Torah*. If the *mitzvah* is observed upon conclusion of the scribal function, then once the last letter is written, the time for the performance of the *mitzvah* is over.

The Talmud (*Rosh HaShanah* 28b) rules that once the requisite time for the observance of a *mitzvah* has concluded, one must have specific intention to observe a *mitzvah* in order to violate *Lo tosef*. A scribe (or owner) who adds an extra letter after the *Sefer Torah* is concluded may not manifest such intention. If, however, as Rabbenu Asher rules, the purpose of the *mitzvah* is to learn Torah, the requisite time for the performance of the mitzvah still prevails even after the last letter has been written. Thus, regardless of intention, *Lo tosef* may be violated.

The major difficulty, as the *Turei Even* himself notes, is the *Sifre*'s position that *Lo tigra* may be transgressed even when one does not observe a *mitzvah* at all. The *Minchat Chinnuch*, quoting the *Turei Even*, concludes that one should not Halachically disagree with the ruling of the *Sifre*. But the *Turei Even* substantiated his view with a Talmudic citation (*Sukkah* 31b). To this the *Sefat Emet* responds that the Talmud relates to a situation where it is impossible to acquire an *etrog*. One does not transgress *Lo tigra* (he rules) in a situation that is beyond one's control (*ones*) (*Sefat Emet, Sukkah* 31b).

13

Ornamentations and Cantillation Notes in a *Sefer Torah*

Many ancient Hebrew texts are elaborately decorated, but *Sifrei Torah* are devoid of ornamentation. It is of interest to determine why this is so, as well as to assess the status of an illuminated *Sefer Torah*.

The *Shulchan Aruch* rules that red, green, and gold lettering cannot be utilized in writing a *Sefer Torah* (*Yoreh De'ah* 271:6). The Shach (ibid.) presents a general rule stipulating that any ink other than black invalidates a *Sefer Torah*. Thus, decorative colors are prohibited, but the assumption that all ornamentation is also prohibited cannot be derived from these laws, because there is a special tradition pertaining to the color of the ink used in writing a *Sefer Torah*.

The *Beit Yosef* (ibid.) cites a Yerushalmi which maintains that the use of a kind of ink called *d'yo* is a Halachah dating back to Moshe Rabbenu (*halachah leMoshe miSinai*), but it is unclear whether *d'yo* refers to a specific substance or to a variety of ingredients which have the same effect. The Rambam, opting for the latter view, suggests that the basis of the *halachah leMoshe* is to disqualify ink of any color other than black (*Hilchot Tefillin*, chap. 1, laws, 4, 5). The *Beit Yosef* concludes that the Rambam's ruling on this matter should be followed. Thus, the use of colors other than black, even though the meaning of the text is not altered, is a deviation which directly violates an ancient tradition. This tradition, however, relates only to the body of the text. It has no bearing on artistic efforts in the margins.

A resolution of the issue may be gleaned from Halachic considerations regarding the marking of cantillations *(trop)* in a *Sefer Torah*. The public reading of a *Sefer Torah* requires the chanting of musical intonations based upon the Masoretic accents known as cantillations (or *trop*). Thus, the reader must memorize not only the correct punctuation of Scripture but also its proper melodic notes. A Halachic question developed in a case where the cantillations were marked in the margins of a *Sefer Torah* to facilitate the proper chanting during public usage. The question was directed to R. Yechezkel Landau, Chief Rabbi of Prague. The basic assumption was that the addition of such notes invalidated the *Sefer Torah*. The concern was whether the *Sefer Torah* was to be permanently disqualified. The basis for this view was the ruling of the *Shulchan Aruch*, which stipulates that a *Sefer Torah* written with punctuation marks is invalid even if the punctuation is erased (*Yoreh De'ah* 274:7). Thus, the inclusion of cantillation notes should be comparable to the rule regarding punctuation, and the *Sefer Torah* in question should be classified as permanently unfit for use.

R. Landau disagrees with this position and presents the following analysis. He cites the *Taz* (*Yoreh De'ah* 274:6), who probes the rationale as to why correcting a punctuated *Sefer Torah* is prohibited but rectifying other textual errors is permitted. The *Taz* contends that a punctuated *Sefer Torah* is invalid because it does not give credence to the concept of *Mesorah*, the cherished oral tradition which guides the proper pronunciation of Biblical words. In a punctuated text, there is no *Mesorah*. Any scribe, suggests the *Taz*, who writes a *Sefer Torah* with punctuation marks seems to be intentionally disregarding and negating the value of *Mesorah*. As a result, such a text can never be used for religious purposes. No subsequent correction or erasure can eliminate the scribe's unholy intentions. This view, suggests R. Landau, is applicable only to the scribe who actually wrote the *Sefer Torah*. In a case, however, where the *Sefer Torah* was written accurately with correct intentions of *kedushah*, the subsequent addition of, for example, cantillation notes would not permanently disqualify the *Sefer Torah*. Once the markings were erased, the *Sefer Torah* would revert to its original status of *kedushah*. Indeed, concludes R. Landau, the only reason why such a *Sefer Torah* is even temporarily unfit for use is that such markings violate the principle of the Ramban, who contends that a *Sefer Torah* must replicate the Torah given on Sinai. That is, nothing whatsoever must be added to the *Sefer Torah* (*Responsa Noda BiYehudah, Mahadura Tinyana, Yoreh De'ah* 172).

Based upon this ruling, any decorative ornamentation of a *Sefer Torah* would disqualify it from usage. Such decorations would be an extraneous addition to a *Sefer Torah* and a deviation from the Ramban's strict rule requiring the authentic reproduction of all *Sifrei Torah*.

Of concern, however, is whether an ornamented *Sefer Torah* would be permanently or only temporarily invalidated. R. Landau permits erasure simply because the cantillation marks were added after the writing of the *Sefer Torah* was concluded. By implication, if the scribe himself had marked the notes in the body of the text while writing the *Sefer Torah*, the *Sefer Torah* would be permanently unfit. Does this rule also apply to scribal ornamentations?

It may be noted that the problem regarding cantillation markings in a *Sefer Torah* can be resolved in a manner quite different from the position of the *Noda BiYehudah*. The *Shulchan Aruch* rules that a *Sefer Torah* with markings indicating the ends of verses is invalid (*Yoreh De'ah* 274:7). The *Taz* (ibid.) notes that the source for this rule is the theory of the Ramban, who requires an accurate replication of the *Sefer Torah* given on Sinai to *Kelal Yisrael* from Moshe Rabbenu. Yet the *Taz* differentiates between this law and the rule which invalidates a punctuated *Sefer Torah*. The latter case involves a fundamental alteration of the text, a change that may even transform the meaning of Scripture. Markings signifying the ends of verses do not alter the meaning of the text. As a result, such errors can be rectified, making the *Sefer Torah* fit for use. The *Gilyon Maharsha* (ibid.) suggests that one may even correct scribal markings in the space between two lines.

Thus, permanent disqualification of a *Sefer Torah* occurs only when additional markings transform the text itself. As a result, cantillation notes would not permanently invalidate a *Sefer Torah*, even if they were originally marked by the scribe during the process of writing the *Sefer Torah*. Decorative illuminations which do not affect the text, therefore, should only temporarily disqualify a *Sefer Torah*, even if the scribe himself created them. However, since scholars contend that cantillation accents frequently provide nuances of meaning to the text itself (see the commentary of the Vilna Gaon), it is plausible to assume that the *Noda BiYehudah* equated the musical accents to punctuation marks. Yet scribal ornamentations may definitely be erased so that the *Sefer Torah* can be properly used.

Once again the purity of the tradition mandates simplicity.

14

Analysis of a Responsum by R. Moshe Feinstein, *Shlita*

THE SIFREI TORAH OF A KING

The discussion in Chapter 1 presented cogent arguments favoring the linkage between the *mitzvah* of writing a *Sefer Torah* and the subsequent donation of the *Sefer Torah* to a synagogue, based upon the premise that loss or diminution of ownership does not invalidate the *mitzvah* of writing a *Sefer Torah*. It should be noted that there is no unanimity of opinion on this issue. Indeed, a great modern sage has taken a contrary position— namely, that the *mitzvah* of writing a *Sefer Torah* mandates continued possession. Thus, someone who donated a *Sefer Torah* to a synagogue would be obligated to write another *Sefer Torah* to fulfill the requirement of the *mitzvah*. Since the sources utilized to corroborate this Halachic position appear somewhat questionable, it is necessary to review the text of the Rambam and the various discussions upon it.

> At the time that a king sits upon the throne of his kingdom [i.e., assumes reign] he writes a *Sefer Torah* for himself in addition to the *Sefer Torah* that his [fore] fathers bequeathed to him. . . . If his forefathers did not bequeath to him [a *Sefer Torah*] or it was lost, he writes two *Sifrei Torah*. One he places in his treasure house, for he is commanded [to have such a *Sefer Torah*] like all [common, i.e., nonroyal] Jews. The second [*Sefer Torah*] should not be apart from him. . . . Should he go to war . . . enter [an assemblage] . . . sit in judgment . . . . it [the *Sefer Torah*] is with him. . . . As Scripture

states, "And it shall be with him and he shall read in it all the days of his life."

(Rambam, *Laws of Kings*, chap. 3, law 1)

The *Kesef Mishneh* notes a difficulty in the terminology of the Rambam. It appears evident that according to the Rambam a king is not always mandated to write two *Sifrei Torah*. This requirement applies only in the event that he has none available (i.e., either not bequeathed to him or lost). However, if the king already has a *Sefer Torah* that was bequeathed to him by his father, he is only required to write one *Sefer Torah*. Why? A commoner may not observe the *mitzvah* of writing a *Sefer Torah* by utilizing a *Sefer Torah* acquired by his parent. Why should a king be different? To overcome this problem, the *Kesef Mishneh* suggests "with difficulty" (*bedochayk*) the following resolution. A king was required to write a personal *Sefer Torah* upon assumption of reign. This obligation could not be fulfilled by using a *Sefer Torah* obtained through inheritance. The king had to personally write this *Sefer Torah* or commission someone to write it for him. As for the other *Sefer Torah*, the one the king was obliged to write in his role as a Jew like other Jews, the king could observe this *mitzvah* by utilizing a *Sefer Torah* acquired through inheritance, even though a commoner may not do so. The reason is that if a commoner could rely upon a *Sefer Torah* inherited from his father, then he would not actually write a *Sefer Torah*, but even if the king does not write the *Sefer Torah* required of him as a Jew like other Jews, he still will write a *Sefer Torah* to fulfill his obligation as a king. As long as one *Sefer Torah* is actually written by the king, it is sufficient.

R. Moshe Feinstein (*Iggrot Mosheh, Orach Chayyim* 52) presents the following analysis of the Rambam and the *Kesef Mishneh*'s theory: The Rambam states that "if his forefathers did not bequeath to him [a *Sefer Torah*] or it was lost, he [the king] writes two *Sifrei Torah*." Logic, at first, would presume that the phrase "it was lost" refers to a *Sefer Torah* written by the king's father. Thus, the Rambam is stating that if a king did not acquire a *Sefer Torah* from his father or he did inherit a *Sefer Torah* and then lost it, he would be required to write another. However, in an instance where the king lost a *Sefer Torah* that he himself had written, perhaps he would not be obliged to write another. The basis for this reasoning is the fact that the Rambam includes the law mandating that a new *Sefer Torah* must be written to replace one that is lost in a phrase dealing primarily with a *Sefer Torah* written by a king's parent. If the Rambam required the rewriting of a *Sefer Torah* in the event that a king lost one that he had himself written, then the Rambam should have included the requirement in a ruling dealing with the laws requiring a king to write a *Sefer Torah* himself.

R. Moshe suggests that such reasoning cannot be substantiated. Indeed, just the opposite position may be deduced from the Rambam: A king must have two *Sifrei Torah*. He must personally write the *Sefer Torah* required of him as a king but according to the *Kesef Mishneh* (previously detailed), he need not personally write the second *Sefer Torah*, the one necessary as a Jew like all Jews. This second *Sefer Torah* may be one inherited from his father. Now assume that the king loses the *Sefer Torah* written by his father. Even if it had been in his possession for many years, the king would still be required to write another *Sefer Torah* to replace it. In other words, the fact that the writing process was completed would not excuse the king from being required to write another *Sefer Torah*. Why? For according to the *Kesef Mishneh* the king need not write this second *Sefer Torah*. His father did. Now if the purpose of the *mitzvah* is merely to write a *Sefer Torah* and not to maintain possession of it, then what is the reason for the king's maintaining a second *Sefer Torah* that he did not write? Also, why is he required to write another if it is lost?

The logical conclusion is that the basic *mitzvah* is continued possession of a *Sefer Torah*. This *mitzvah* has a conditional aspect that the *Sefer Torah* must be personally written and not received from a parent. According to the Rambam, this condition does not apply to a king who meets his obligation to write a *Sefer Torah* by writing the royal *Sefer Torah*. But the king must retain possession of the commoner's *Sefer Torah*, because continued ownership is an integral aspect of the *mitzvah*. Therefore, the loss of either *Sefer Torah*, whether the one written by the king's father or the one he wrote himself, mandates the writing of another *Sefer Torah*. Thus, the Rambam is the source for the position that continued possession of a *Sefer Torah* is a key element of the *mitzvah* of writing a *Sefer Torah*.

Though R. Moshe's incisive, probing questions require a response, it may be shown, with great reverence for his sagacity and scholarship, that his conclusions are not necessarily substantiated.

Basic to the issue is comprehension of the *Kesef Mishneh's* theory. This position, not necessarily held by all scholars, maintains that a king may observe the *mitzvah* of a *Sefer Torah* required of him in his capacity as a Jew like all Jews by utilizing a *Sefer Torah* inherited from his father. If the king fulfills his obligation to write a *Sefer Torah* by writing the *Sefer Torah* required of him as a king, he need not actually write the commoner's *Sefer Torah*.

An analysis of this position suggests the following orientation. A king has a special *mitzvah* to write a *Sefer Torah* upon assumption of reign, but he is also required to observe the *mitzvot* incumbent upon all Jews. Since all Jews must write a *Sefer Torah*, the king must also write a *Sefer Torah*.

The basic question is whether a king actually needs two *Sifrei Torah*. Couldn't it be maintained that his general (nonroyal) *mitzvah* is observed by his act of writing the royal *Sefer Torah*? And if this is so, then one *Sefer Torah* would suffice to meet both obligations. Since the general consensus held that both *Sifrei Torah* were Halachically kosher, it appears illogical to require a king to maintain two *Sifrei Torah*. Indeed, if the general (nonroyal) *mitzvah* was to actually write a *Sefer Torah* (and not maintain it), then the process of writing the royal *Sefer Torah* should simultaneously fulfill both *mitzvot*.

This is the rationale for the *Kesef Mishneh*. For this reason the king was only required to write one royal *Sefer Torah*. Yet if this be so, reasons R. Moshe, why did he need the second *Sefer Torah* at all? It is possible that in terms of the requirement of all nonroyal Jews, the king fulfilled his *mitzvah* by writing his royal *Sefer Torah*. But there is a special nuance associated with the royal *Sefer Torah*. Scripture states, "and he shall write a *mishneh Torah*," which Hirsch literally yet correctly translates as "a double copy of this Torah" (Deuteronomy 17:18). In other words, the king's *Sefer Torah* was mandated by Scripture to be a "second one." It had to be an additional *Sefer Torah*—something in addition to the one he already had. Thus, the possession of the general, nonroyal *Sefer Torah* was not in any way related to the general *mitzvah*. It was necessary so that the royal *Sefer Torah* could be the second *Sefer Torah* (*mishneh Torah*). Therefore, the Rambam says that if a king had no *Sefer Torah* available, he had to write two *Sifrei Torah*. The first, the Rambam states, is the general *Sefer Torah*. In other words, when a king needed to write two *Sifrei Torah*, the first could not be his royal *Sefer Torah*. To the extent that the whole purpose of two *Sifrei Torah* was merely so that the royal one could be the second, there was no requirement to write both. Thus, the first *Sefer Torah* could be one acquired through inheritence. The implication was that the royal *Sefer Torah* should be unique, unequivocally recognizable as something required only of royalty. If a king had only one *Sefer Torah*, the royal *Sefer Torah* would not be special. Therefore, the *Sefer Torah* that the king possessed in his capacity as a Jew like all Jews had no purpose except to highlight the uniqueness of the second.

This interpretation, apart from its logical component, is clearly inferred from the terse summary of the Rambam's rulings by the *Kiryat Sefer* (Mabit). He states, "If he had none from his forefathers [i.e., if the king had no *Sefer Torah* bequeathed to him] he writes two, as Scripture states, *mishneh*, which means 'two' " (*Laws of Kings*, chap. 3). Note also the Meiri (*Sanhedrin* 21), who rules "that the *Sefer Torah* of the king was not just *mishneh Torah* [Deuteronomy] but a complete Torah comparable to the one in his treasury house. The term *mishneh Torah* means second to the one in his treasury house." In other words, if not for this specific Biblical term, the king would not be obligated to write two *Sifrei Torah*. As a result, it is apparent that the king's two *Sifrei Torah* were governed by rules distinctly different from those pertaining to the *Sefer Torah* required of a commoner. This makes it evident that a generalized ruling cannot be derived from the laws dealing with either or both of the king's *Sifrei Torah*.

PURCHASING A SEFER TORAH

R. Moshe Feinstein contends that there is conclusive documentation to support the Halachic theory that continued ownership of a *Sefer Torah* is an integral aspect of the *mitzvah*. To the extent that this so-called great substantiation is based upon an interpretation of commentaries of Talmudic and early sources, it is necessary to review the basic texts in order to properly analyze the issue.

> The Talmud states (*Menachot* 30a): "R. Yehoshua bar Abba said in the name of R. Giddal, who said in the name of Rav, 'Acquiring a *Sefer Torah* from the market is considered as if he grabbed [*chataf*] a *mitzvah* from the market; should he write it [a *Sefer Torah*], Scripture deems it as if he accepted [the Torah] from Sinai'; R. Sheshet said that if he corrects even one letter, it is considered as if he wrote it."

Tosafot notes that R. Sheshet refers to an instance wherein one acquired a *Sefer Torah* from the market. Correcting a letter, suggests Tosafot, is not in the same category as "having grabbed a *mitzvah*"; for the case wherein a *Sefer Torah* had to be corrected implies that the seller committed a sin by maintaining in his possession a *Sefer Torah* not valid for usage.

The *Mordechai* (*Hilchot Ketanot* 957), in an apparent attempt to clarify the position of Tosafot, makes the following remarks: One who corrects even one letter of a *Sefer Torah* is not considered as if he "grabbed a *mitzvah* from the market," for the process of correcting the *Sefer Torah* did not diminish the *mitzvah* of his friend (the seller), but just the opposite: the seller (by maintaining in his possession a *Sefer Torah* that was invalid for usage [*pasul*]) committed a sin, and the buyer, by fixing the *Sefer*

Torah (and making it valid) removed the sin from the seller. (This position is also reported by the *Darchei Mosheh* in his notes to the *Tur Shulchan Aruch, Yoreh De'ah* 270. The *Derishah* [ibid.] notes a source contending that the buyer is a thief. R. Moshe contends that this source is the position of the *Mordechai*.)

In other words, suggests R. Moshe, a person who buys a *Sefer Torah* is considered as if he "grabbed a *mitzvah*," for he diminished the *mitzvah* of the seller. If so, this means that a seller loses his *mitzvah* by selling a *Sefer Torah*. (The reason must be that by the sale the seller removed the *Sefer Torah* from his possession and ownership, which is an act that invalidates the *mitzvah*.) Now if selling a *Sefer Torah* causes the seller to lose his *mitzvah*, then donating a *Sefer Torah* to a synagogue should have the same effect on the donor's *mitzvah*, "for what difference is there between selling a *Sefer Torah* and donating it to a synagogue?" Though R. Moshe notes that the *Derishah* and other scholars have great difficulty in equating a buyer with a thief, he rules that "the position of the *Mordechai* that the seller diminishes his *mitzvah* by the sale is the general Halachic consensus without any disagreement."

R. Moshe further notes that a lost or stolen *Sefer Torah* may be in a different category than one which is sold, for in the former instances the owner still maintains ownership and only lacks possession. As a result, no generalization applying to lost or stolen *Sifrei Torah* may be derived from the laws dealing with buying or selling a *Sefer Torah*.

R. Moshe suggests that the source that requires a person who loses a *Sefer Torah* to write another is the ruling of the Rambam that mandates a king to write another *Sefer Torah* upon such a loss even if the *Sefer Torah* is still in use by another. Yet R. Moshe concludes that the donation of a *Sefer Torah* to a synagogue definitely invalidates the *mitzvah*.

To verify the validity of R. Moshe's position, it is necessary to review once again the Talmudic citation and the basic commentaries and Halachot. The Talmud (*Menachot* 30a) presents three cases.

1. Purchasing a *Sefer Torah* is considered the same as "grabbing a *mitzvah*."
2. Writing a *Sefer Torah* is considered the same as receiving it from Mount Sinai.
3. Correcting a *Sefer Torah* is considered the same as writing it.

Commenting on the first case, Rashi notes that the phrase describing the purchaser as one who "grabbed a *mitzvah*" means that while the act of purchasing does indeed grant a *mitzvah* to the purchaser, he who writes a *Sefer Torah* acquires a greater *mitzvah*. The distinction is that the writing of a *Sefer Torah* entails greater effort, and therefore provides a greater reward (see *Beit Yosef, Tur Yoreh De'ah* 270). Tosafot suggests that the third case refers to an instance of purchase; i.e., someone bought an invalid *Sefer Torah* and corrected it. Tosafot states that one who buys and corrects a *Sefer Torah* is not in the same category as one who "grabbed a *mitzvah*," for the person who sold the *Sefer Torah* had committed a sin by previously retaining a *Sefer Torah* that required correction.

A simple interpretation is that Tosafot does not disagree with Rashi's Halachic ruling that the purchase of a *Sefer Torah* vests the buyer with the *mitzvah* of writing a *Sefer Torah*. The Talmudic phrase that a purchaser "grabbed a *mitzvah*" appears to have a negative connotation. It suggests that anyone so labeled is on a lower level than one who actually writes a *Sefer Torah*. So Tosafot wishes to emphasize that a person who buys and subsequently corrects a *Sefer Torah* is not to be categorized with the negative phrase but, rather, is to be placed on the positive plateau of one who wrote a *Sefer Torah*. The reason is that the purchaser by his correction has expended effort and simultaneously rescued the seller from the sin of maintaining an unkosher *Sefer Torah*. Tosafot is, therefore, an additional commentary which in no way disputes Rashi's ruling that a purchaser observes the *mitzvah*.

1. R. Moshe Isserles (Rama, *Shulchan Aruch* 270) ruled that

anyone who purchases a *Sefer Torah* and does not correct it is considered as if he "grabbed a *mitzvah* from the market" and does not observe the *mitzvah*. The Vilna Gaon, however, notes that the Halachah is as Rashi reported in *Menachot* 30a. In other words, a purchaser observes the *mitzvah* even if he does not correct one letter.

In analyzing this Halachah, the *Aruch HaShulchan* (ibid.) simply cannot comprehend the basis for the Rama's ruling. Indeed, the *Aruch HaShulchan* reports the positions of both Rashi and Tosafot and contends that Tosafot presents an additive commentary which does not dispute the basic Halachah that a purchaser of a *Sefer Torah* observes the *mitzvah*. He suggests that the Rambam, by the very fact that he excludes any reference to acquiring a *mitzvah* through a purchase, may be the source of the Rama's ruling. Yet the practical law, he concludes, is the position of Rashi, as ruled by the Vilna Gaon. What then is the basis of the Rama's decision? To the extent that the Rama, in his commentary, the *Darchei Moshe*, presents the view of the *Mordechai* that a purchaser diminishes the *mitzvah* of the seller, this must be the source of his subsequent ruling that a purchaser does not observe the *mitzvah* at all. The Rama must be of the opinion that one cannot observe the *mitzvah* if the process of acquiring the *Sefer Torah* in some way diminished the *mitzvah* for another. To the extent that Rashi disagrees with this position, it must mean that Rashi believes that a purchaser does not detract at all from the previous *mitzvah* of the seller. If so, then there is a Halachic debate between the *Mordechai* and Rashi as to whether continued ownership is vital to the *mitzvah* of writing a *Sefer Torah*. The Rama ruled in favor of the *Mordechai*, and the Vilna Gaon ruled in support of Rashi. The *Aruch HaShulchan* also favors Rashi's position. As a result, R. Moshe's contention that no one disputes the *Mordechai*'s position is incredible.

2. A possible response is that there are two distinct factors involved in the sale of a *Sefer Torah*: (1) The seller loses his *mitzvah* by virtue of the sale, for he has removed the *Sefer Torah* from his possession—this is the position of the *Mordechai*, who

categorizes such a process as having "grabbed a *mitzvah* from the market." (2) The buyer does not acquire the *mitzvah*, for a *mitzvah* cannot be observed by depriving someone else of a *mitzvah*—this is the Rama's position. Rashi, however, may agree with the *Mordechai* yet disagree with the Rama. This means that Rashi agrees with the ruling that a seller loses his *mitzvah*, since continued possession of a *Sefer Torah* is essential to the *mitzvah*, but does not believe that such a process invalidates the *mitzvah* of the buyer. Accordingly, the status of the buyer's *mitzvah* is in no way affected by the problems of the seller. Thus, the *Mordechai's* position would not be disputed by Rashi.

This orientation would certainly be a forced interpretation of Rashi. Indeed, Rashi does not relate to any problems of the seller. The reason why Rashi rules that a purchaser is on a lower level than one who writes a *Sefer Torah* is, as previously noted by the *Beit Yosef* (*Yoreh De'ah* 270), that the act of purchasing a *Sefer Torah* requires less effort than the act of writing one. Therefore, greater reward is granted to one who writes (or commissions the writing of) an entire *Sefer Torah*. This interpretation overtly suggests that the phrase "grabbed a *mitzvah* from the market" has nothing to do with the seller. That is, the seller's *mitzvah* is not affected by the sale. The sole problem is the minimum effort of the buyer.

If Rashi agrees with the *Mordechai*, he should have delineated some concern about the seller's *mitzvah*. The total absence of such concern suggests that Rashi does not impugn the status of the seller's *mitzvah*.

3. The *Derishah* (commentary on *Tur Shulchan Aruch, Yoreh De'ah* 270) reports a theory that defines the phrase "grabbed a *mitzvah* from the market" to mean that the purchaser is a thief who robbed the *mitzvah* from the seller. R. Moshe notes that the *Derishah* is not content with this definition, for the buyer committed no crime by purchasing a *Sefer Torah* willingly sold by the seller. Yet he (R. Moshe) still contends that no one disputes the position that a buyer detracts from the *mitzvah* of the seller.

This appears to be overtly contrary to the *Derishah,* who notes that the Talmudic text states that a purchaser is one who "grabbed a *mitzvah* from the market." If the purchaser is one who robbed (or even detracted from the seller's *mitzvah*), reasons the *Derishah,* then the text should have said that such a person is one "who grabbed a *mitzvah* from his friend." Since the text does not in any way refer to the seller's *mitzvah,* the *Derishah* concludes that this previous position is incorrect. Thus, the *Derishah* is explicitly stating that the Talmud is in no way discussing the seller's loss of a *mitzvah.* This is an open challenge to the *Mordechai.* As a result of such logic, moreover, the *Derishah* contends that Rashi's position is valid. In other words, the *Derishah* maintains that Rashi disagrees with the previous theory.

The *Derishah* further notes as a possible explanation of the phrase "he grabbed a *mitzvah*" that the purchaser accomplished nothing by his purchase. He made no alteration in the *Sefer Torah* itself. What difference does it make to the *Sefer Torah* whether it is owned by the seller or the buyer? This suggests a new approach to the *mitzvah.* It implies that to acquire the *mitzvah* of writing a *Sefer Torah* it is necessary to actually write something in the *Sefer Torah.* This may be the basis for the Rama's ruling that the purchase of a *Sefer Torah* does not entitle one to observe the *mitzvah.* This, of course, has no relationship to the theory that continued ownership is vital to the *mitzvah.*

4. R. Moshe contends that if a seller of a *Sefer Torah* loses his *mitzvah,* then one who donates a *Sefer Torah* to a synagogue should be in the same category. This logic is certainly not conclusive. There is a major difference between selling a *Sefer Torah* and donating it to a synagogue. R. Akiva Eiger (*Yoreh De'ah* 270) reports the position of the *Torat Chayyim* that the donation of a *Sefer Torah* to a synagogue invalidates the *mitzvah* and requires the donor to write another one. Commenting on this position, R. Akiva Eiger suggests that accordingly a *Sefer Torah* may not be written by partners. The reason is that a person who donates a *Sefer Torah* to a synagogue does not relinquish total ownership. He is deemed to be a partner comparable to

the other members of the congregation. Thus, there is a logical distinction between a *Sefer Torah* that is sold and one that is donated to a synagogue. Even if one assumed that the sale of a *Sefer Torah* invalidated the *mitzvah,* one could not generalize the assumption that the same principle applies when a *Sefer Torah* is donated to a synagogue; for in the latter case an element of ownership is retained.

5. To the extent that the preceding extensive analysis has demonstrated that the Rambam's rulings relating to the requirement of a king do not apply to any law of a commoner, there is no basis for the position that a lost or stolen *Sefer Torah* invalidates the *mitzvah.*

Thus, it is evident that the so-called conclusive substantiation supporting the Halachic hypothesis that continued ownership or possession of a *Sefer Torah* is vital to the performance of the *mitzvah* of writing a *Sefer Torah* is simply not verified. Consequently, the *mitzvah* of writing a *Sefer Torah* is in no way jeopardized by any subsequent donation to a synagogue. Just the opposite; such a donation (as previously noted) is a lofty extension of the *mitzvah.* As a result, there is no Halachic necessity to limit the terms of the grant to a *synagogue* or institution.

To the extent, however, that a number of rabbinical authorities support the position that continued ownership is necessary for the *mitzvah,* a pragmatic Halachic resolution would be to observe all rulings, even those not substantiated, so that the *mitzvah* can be accomplished without even a scintilla of doubt. This means that the donor should expressly retain ownership of the *Sefer Torah* and provide the synagogue with full access to use. This practice would be a means of *Kavod HaTorah* to the sage R. Moshe and others. The Maharsham notes that even though the common practice may be to consider the *mitzvah* to be observed upon conclusion of the writing process, one should not disregard the position of those who disagree (see *Responsa Maharsham,* vol. 1, 48; also *Da'at Torah,* vol. II, responsum 71).

It should be noted that this suggestion is applicable only in the event that an individual writes a *Sefer Torah*, or commissions a scribe to write one, solely for himself, and therefore retains ownership as a pragmatic strategy to ensure that his *mitzvah* is observed, not merely according to general or majority opinion, but according to unanimous rulings of Halachic sages. Retention of ownership in this instance is simply a means of providing unanimous consent for his action. When a *Sefer Torah* is written through a process of joint partnership, however, retention of ownership is totally unnecessary. Indeed, it would be based upon personal whim rather than Halachic rulings.

When a jointly owned *Sefer Torah* is given to a synagogue, the number of parties to the partnership is, in effect, being increased. The donor does not relinquish all elements of ownership. He merely increases the number of partners. He is still a part-owner comparable to other members of the congregation. Those who disallow the use of partnership for the *mitzvah* of writing a *Sefer Torah* make no distinction between two partners and one thousand partners. As a result, retention of ownership in such a case has no Halachic basis (see R. Akiva Eiger, op. cit.).

15

The Talmudic Source for Rabbenu Asher's Theory and Its Halachic Implications

THE SOURCE FOR RABBENU ASHER'S THEORY

Rabbenu Asher ruled that learning Torah is the purpose of the *mitzvah* of writing a *Sefer Torah*. That is, the *Sefer Torah* is to be a text from which Torah may be studied.

Though this theory is discussed by numerous commentaries and even codified into law (*Yoreh De'ah* 270), there does not appear to be any analysis relating to the source material for it. The only approach has been to note that Scripture appears to sustain this theory (see ibid.), yet it is a general guideline of Halachah that practical rulings are to be based upon concepts rooted in Talmudic citations. Thus, it is necessary to seek out the textual support for Rabbenu Asher's theory.

It is suggested that a report in the Yerushalmi may serve as the basis for this concept. Discussing the royal *Sefer Torah*, the Yerushalmi (*Sanhedrin* 13a) states:

> And when he [the king] goes to war, it [the *Sefer Torah*] is with him, as Scripture states: "and it shall be with him, and he shall read therein all the days of his life" [Deuteronomy 17:19]. Now [this is a *kal vachomer*], if a Jewish king who is involved in the [communal] needs of [*Kelal*] *Yisrael*, the Torah says of him "that he shall read Torah all the days of his life," a commoner must certainly [be obligated to] do so. Similarly, of Yehoshua [Joshua] Scripture states,

"and he shall dwell in it day and night" [*Vehagita bo yomam valaylah*];
[this also is a *kal vachomer*] if the Torah mandates Yehoshua, who is
involved in [communal] needs of [*Kelal*] *Yisrael*, with such a requirement, is not a common Jew so mandated?

From the quotation given above it is apparent that the
Jerusalem Talmud specifically contends that the role of a commoner may be derived from the mandate of a king. Just as a
king is required to "read therein," which, of course, means, to
learn in his royal *Sefer Torah*, so too must a commoner learn
from his personal *Sefer Torah*. Indeed, that is the distinction
between this and the latter case. In the former illustration the
discussion relates to utilizing the *Sefer Torah* as a text for Torah
study. In the latter case, the discussion refers to the general
principle of learning Torah, without any reference to the specific text required. Thus, this may be the source for the theory
of Rabbenu Asher.

The difficulty with this position is that laws pertaining to a
king are unique and generally pertain only to royalty. Indeed, a
king is mandated to constantly manifest the presence of a *Sefer
Torah* through all his pursuits. As the Babylonian Talmud
(*Sanhedrin* 21b) notes, the royal *Sefer Torah* has to be present no
matter what the king is doing—whether engaging in war,
sitting in judgment, or attending an assemblage. At no time is
there any discussion suggesting that a commoner is similarly
required to have his *Sefer Torah* present at all times, yet it is
possible to present a convincing argument that such an obligation derives from the laws relating to a king. Why did the
Talmud not say that just as a king, who is preoccupied with the
communal problems of *Kelal Yisrael*, is required to manifest the
presence of a *Sefer Torah*, so too should a common Jew? The
basic reply to this question is that general laws cannot be
derived from statutes dealing with royalty. A king has a unique
status, and Scripture by fiat has afforded him certain distinct
benefits and obligations. This being so, it is not valid to deduce
the purpose of the *mitzvah* of writing a *Sefer Torah* from the rules
relating to a king. Yet the Yerushalmi does, in fact, make such a

comparison. It is, therefore, necessary to determine why only certain laws may be derived from the rules relating to a king— and others may not.

In a discussion of the royal *Sefer Torah* which the king must constantly have present with him, the Talmud states (Babylonian Talmud, *Sanhedrin* 21b):

> This [*Sefer Torah*] did not accompany the king when he entered a bathhouse or toilet facilities, for Scripture reads, "And it shall be with him and he shall read therein." [Only] in a place wherein he may read therein.

The *Sefer Torah* is therefore required to accompany the king only in an area where reading of the Torah is permissible. Since one does not read the Torah in certain places the *Sefer Torah* is not to be present at such times.

R. Yaakov Ettinger (commentary on *Sanhedrin* 21b, *Aruch LaNer*) presents the following analysis: The Talmud exempts the presence of a *Sefer Torah* in the above-mentioned locations on the basis of the Scriptural verse which places the requirement of reading the *Sefer Torah* adjacent to the phrase mandating constant presence. The context suggests that the *Sefer Torah* is not to be present when one is not reading or learning Torah. Yet even without this Scriptural reference it may be determined that one should not bring a *Sefer Torah* to such places. The Talmud (*Shabbat* 22a) notes a general principle that one is not permitted to denigrate (shame) *mitzvot*. On the basis of this principle, bringing *tefillin* into toilet facilities is prohibited, because the sanctity of the *tefillin* would be debased and denigrated in such places. Since a *Sefer Torah* certainly has a greater degree of *kedushah* than *tefillin*, it is not permitted to bring a *Sefer Torah* into such a place. Thus there is no necessity for a specific Scriptural reference excluding a royal *Sefer Torah* from such facilities.

To clarify this matter R. Yaakov Ettinger notes that Scripture presents three distinct phrases relating to the royal *Sefer Torah*. It is written: (1) "And it shall be with him"; (2) "and he shall read therein"; (3) "all the days of his life" (Deuteronomy 17:19). The third phrase, "all the days of his life," must relate to the first clause, which mandates the constant presence of a *Sefer Torah*. Thus, Scripture is articulating the view that the presence of the *Sefer Torah* must be a constant factor all the days of the king's life. Indeed, the third clause does not relate to the requirement of the king to read (i.e., learn from) the royal *Sefer Torah* constantly. The reason is that it would be impossible to observe such a requirement. (It is impractical to assume that a king has a constant, continual mandate to study from his royal *Sefer Torah*, for such a *mitzvah* would preclude a king from attending to his royal, communal obligations.) Indeed, while the daily *mitzvah* of recounting the Exodus from Egypt is based upon Scripture, which mandates that "thou mayest remember the day when thou came forth out of the land of Egypt *all the days of your life*" (*Berachot* 12b; Deuteronomy 16:3), there is no requirement to remember the Exodus constantly throughout the day. Such a requirement would be impractical and impossible to observe properly. As a result, the Biblical mandate is followed by merely mentioning the Exodus once by day and once by night. There is no requirement (for the king) to read in his royal *Sefer Torah* once by day and once at night. Why not? Simply because the clause "all the days of his life" does not relate to the mandate to read the royal *Sefer Torah* but to the phrase requiring that the *Sefer Torah* be a constant appendage of the king.

As a result, the Talmud was originally of the opinion that the mandate of the continual presence of the royal *Sefer Torah* superseded all other rules—even those which prohibited bringing holy items into such places as toilet facilities and bath-houses. To this supposition, the Talmud notes the context of the Scriptural mandate. If the clause "all the days of his life" does not relate to the requirement of learning in a royal *Sefer Torah*, then why does Scripture state, "and it shall be with him, and he shall learn therein, all the days of his life"? Should not Scripture have arranged the components of the verse differently and stated, "and he shall learn therein, and it shall be with him, all the days of his life"? This would make it evident that learning in the royal *Sefer Torah* has no relationship to the ruling that it must be all the days of the king's life. To this the Talmud responds that the mandate to read in the *Sefer Torah* is placed after the rule requiring the presence of the *Sefer Torah* to teach us that when the *Sefer Torah* is not read, there is no requirement to have it present.

The analysis of the *Aruch LaNer* suggests unique insights into the *mitzvah*, even though his conclusions need not be accepted. Scripture states: (1) "and it shall be with him," (2) "and he shall read therein," (3) "all the days of his life." The third clause may relate to both previous rulings. As it pertains to the physical presence of the *Sefer Torah* as an appendage of the king, the clause "all the days of his life" may suggest a constant, continual factor. As a result, the Talmud believed that it may supersede even such prohibitions as the one against bringing a *Sefer Torah* into a bathhouse. Yet as it relates to the *mitzvah* of the king using his *Sefer Torah* as a text, it may, indeed, be factual that the *mitzvah* is comparable to recounting the story of the Exodus from Egypt. Indeed, whenever Scripture uses the phrase "all the days of your [or his] life," it is necessary to determine whether the requirement is practical or not. Whenever the requirement does not preclude engaging in normal activities, the ruling is exact and constant performance is required, as in the instance of the royal *Sefer Torah* being constantly with the king. On the other hand, whenever the ruling would inhibit normal activities, it is not taken literally and relates only to a minimum observance, once by day and once by night.

This then may be the meaning of the citation in the Jerusalem Talmud. A king is only obliged to learn in his royal *Sefer Torah* once by day and once by night. He is not required to constantly learn Torah, for such a mandate would be impractical. Thus he is granted a minimum obligation to learn Torah. Now if a king, who has communal obligations to *Kelal Yisrael*, is required to learn in his royal *Sefer Torah* at least once by day and once by night, should not a common Jew have the same minimal obligation? In other words, the mandate requiring the king to read in his royal *Sefer Torah* is not a special added *mitzvah* afforded to a king. It is, rather, a leniency granted him to limit the observance. This limitation of minimum obligation pertains as much to a common Jew as to a king. As a result, the charge may not be sustained that such a law applies only to a king.

Indeed, as it pertains to Torah study itself, the *general* obligation of the common Jew is derived from a mandate issued to a leader who ostensibly served in a role comparable to that of a King. Joshua, who replaced Moshe Rabbenu as the sole leader of *Kelal Yisrael*, surely enjoyed a status comparable to that of a king. Thus the Yerushalmi notes: "of Yehoshua, Scripture states, 'and he shall dwell in it day and night' [*Vehagita bo yomam velaylah*]. Now if the Torah mandates Yehoshua, who is involved in the [communal] needs of [*Kelal*] *Yisrael*, with such a requirement, is not a common Jew so mandated?" (Jerusalem Talmud, *Sanhedrin* 13a). Why did the Jerusalem Talmud cite this case in a discussion dealing with the *mitzvah* of the royal *Sefer Torah*? Perhaps the Yerushalmi was seeking to substantiate the view that in regard to Torah study, the requirement of a common Jew may be derived from laws dealing with a king. It is evident that the requirement of *Vehagita bo* was directed solely to Yehoshua. Yet everyone is in accord with the view that the mandate is applicable to all Jews. Why? Because even that mandate (*Vehagita bo*) has a minimum requirement. The Talmud (*Menachot* 99b) notes that even if a Jew learns only one chapter in the morning and another in the evening, this would be sufficient to meet the minimum requirement of the mandate. (Note that the Yerushalmi quotes the latter part of the verse, while the Babylonian Talmud quotes the former part.) Thus Yehoshua, who was preoccupied with communal obligations, was still required to learn Torah at least once by day and once by night. It is logical to assume that the same minimum requirement applies to all Jews. Thus, the minimum standards of Torah study may be derived from rulings related to a king. Indeed, it may be demonstrated that the *mitzvah* of learning Torah day and night (*Vehagita bo*) and the *mitzvah* of writing a *Sefer Torah* are closely intertwined.

The Talmud (*Berachot* 13a) cites an ancient debate as to whether "the entire Torah was only in the holy tongue." Rashi contends that this relates to *Keri'at HaTorah*. In other words, *Keri'at HaTorah* must only be in the Hebrew language. Tosafot notes that since the debate relates to Biblical verses and *Keri'at HaTorah* is not a Biblical law, the statement must refer only to the Biblical mandate to read *Parashat Zachor* or to the few cases where certain Biblical portions must be quoted, such as for *Bikkurim* ("first fruits"). The commentary *Siftei Chachamim* (ibid.) notes that the position of Tosafot does not mesh with the Talmudic text which states that "*the entire Torah* was in the holy tongue." This suggests a more expanded role than the limited position of Tosafot. The Meiri, however, suggests a most unique interpretation of the statement. He maintains that the debate concerns the *mitzvah* of learning Torah (derived from the verse *Vehagita bo*). Those who hold that the entire Torah is in the holy tongue contend that Torah must be learned only in Hebrew. Those who say that the entire Torah is not in the holy tongue maintain that Torah learning does not need the *kedushah* of Hebrew.

The following is a basic clarification of this position: It is necessary to determine the rationale for any insistence that Torah learning is limited to the Hebrew language. Perhaps the concern is that Torah should be studied in an aura of *kedushah*. This suggests, perhaps, that Torah learning must be from a text that has *Kedushat Sefer Torah*. It is not sufficient just to learn Torah. Rather, it is necessary that the process be one which involves the *kedushah* of a *Sefer Torah*. The Biblical requirement to learn Torah day and night may have originally been restricted to the utilization of a *Sefer Torah*.

The accepted mandate obligating Torah study by day and by night is the verse *vehagita bo*, but this verse is in the Book of Joshua, not in the Pentateuch. As a result, it certainly cannot be the ultimate source for a Biblical *mitzvah*. If so, then what is the Biblical source necessitating Torah study by day and by night?

In *Berachot* 21a there is a debate concerning the nature of *Keri'at Shema*. Some say that it is a Biblical command, and others that it is only a rabbinical ordinance. To those who contend that the *Shema* is a rabbinical mandate, an objection was raised noting that Scripture appears to sustain a contrary position, for the Bible says, "and you shall talk of them . . . when you retire [at night] and rise up [in the morning]." This verse clearly suggests that every Jew must say the words of the *Shema* each evening and morning. Thus, the *Shema* must certainly be a Biblical *mitzvah*. To this charge the Talmud retorts that those who maintain that the chanting of the *Shema* is a rabbinical requirement would interpret the Scriptural verse as relating to Torah study.

The *Shagot Aryeh* (responsum no. 1) presents the following clarification. If the Bible is referring to Torah study, then it is obligating the Jew to learn Torah at least once at night and once by day. The choice of the text to be studied is totally within the discretion of the student. As long as he studies a Torah portion by day and by night, he may select either the portion of the *Shema* or any other Biblical portion to meet his requirement. Those, however, who subscribe to the viewpoint that the *Shema* is a Biblical *mitzvah* would contend that the Scripture is not mandating a general requirement but a specific textual assignment to be chanted twice a day—namely, the *Shema*.

Since the mainstream of Halachah has ruled that the saying of the *Shema* is a Biblical *mitzvah*, the above-quoted verse specifically relates only to the reading of the *Shema*. Hence, there is no source that obligates learning Torah by day and by night.

This then is the import of the citation in the Jerusalem Talmud:

1. Scripture notes that "he [the king] shall read therein [in the royal *Sefer Torah*] all the days of his life." This suggests that the requirement is but once by day and once by night (similar to the *mitzvah* of recounting the Exodus).
2. All Jews are required to possess a *Sefer Torah*.
3. If a king with his manifold obligations must learn Torah at least twice each day, so must the common Jew.

4. The royal requirement to learn Torah was only through the vehicle of a *Sefer Torah*. The commoner was also so obliged.

5. The Scriptural mandate to Joshua, "and you shall dwell therein day and night" (*Vehagita bo*), was an expansion of the mandate in the Pentateuch. It was no longer necessary to learn Torah from a *Sefer Torah*. The knowledge studied and comprehended, rather than the text from which it was studied, was considered the essence of Torah learning. This was a radical departure from the original mandate, which required an object of *kedushah*.

6. This may be the historical reason why Torah was no longer studied from *Sifrei Torah*. As the *mitzvah* expanded—with the shift of emphasis from the process of textual study to the knowledge and comprehension of Torah material—*Sifrei Torah* lost their basic *raison d'être* for the average Jew.

7. As the *mitzvah* of learning Torah was expanded, so too was the *mitzvah* of writing a *Sefer Torah*. Since Torah may be learned from any text, the *Sefer Torah mitzvah* was expanded (according to Rabbenu Asher) to include the writing of any text that facilitates Torah study.

MUST RELIGIOUS TEXTS BE WRITTEN OR PURCHASED?

The concept elaborated in the preceding section serves as the rationale for yet another Halachic problem. As we have explained, Rabbenu Asher formulated the theory that in our time the *mitzvah* of writing a *Sefer Torah* may be observed by writing a religious text like the Mishnah or the Talmud (loc. cit.). Accordingly, it must be determined whether actually writing such a text (or commissioning someone to write it) is required, or whether it may be acquired by means of purchase. In other words, is the process of writing essential to the *mitzvah*, or is it sufficient simply to own religious texts for the purpose of Torah study?

The *Sefer HaChinnuch* (*mitzvah* 613) and the *Derishah* (*Yoreh De'ah* 270) note that one may purchase such texts, but the *Tur*

(*Yoreh De'ah* 270) relates only to the writing and does not mention the purchase of such items.

The *Shulchan Aruch* (*Yoreh De'ah* 270) states, "In our time there is a *mitzvah* to write such texts as the Pentateuch [i.e., not in the form of a *Sefer Torah*], Mishnah, Gemara, and its commentaries." This Halachah is presented without any remarks by the Rama, which suggests that the Rama agrees with the ruling of R. Yosef Caro. Yet the Rama specifically invalidated the *mitzvah* of a *Sefer Torah* acquired through the vehicle of a purchase (ibid.). If so, then why did the Rama not note that religious texts cannot be acquired by means of a purchase?

Two interpretations are suggested:

1. The Rama may be of the opinion that the terminology of the *Shulchan Aruch* is to be understood literally. That is, the codes state that such religious texts must be "written." Thus, the purchasing of religious texts does not vest the buyer with the *mitzvah*. As a result, no comment is necessary. This would suggest that the general debate as to whether the *mitzvah* of a *Sefer Torah* may be acquired through a purchase also applies to the acquisition of religious texts.
2. Since purchasing such texts is the usual custom (and there is no insistence on actually writing them), a completely different approach is needed. As previously detailed, the *mitzvah* of learning Torah was expanded to include all Torah knowledge regardless of text. In other words, Torah learning was no longer intertwined with the *kedushah* of a *Sefer Torah*. The insistence on having a *Sefer Torah* written was only as a means of ensuring the *kedushah* of a *Sefer Torah*. Once Torah learning was separated from the necessity of *Kedushat Sefer Torah*, it was no longer important to require the actual process of writing. As a result, religious texts may be purchased even according to the position of the Rama.

It should be noted, however, that some of the original limitations on the *Sefer Torah mitzvah* may be applicable to the process of acquiring religious texts. One, for example, is the stipulation that the *mitzvah* is not vested to an heir. Thus, it is logical to assume that inheriting a library of religious texts would not be a way of observing the *mitzvah*. The purpose of the *mitzvah* is to facilitate Torah study, but inheriting texts would militate against this, because it would limit the number of texts actually used. Thus, every Jew is required to personally expend effort to obtain religious texts. In order to ensure involvement with the *mitzvah*, this is mandatory even if one already owns a library of inherited books. Of course, acquiring a library of religious texts simply for aesthetic and decorative purposes (and not to learn Torah) would not be an observance of the *mitzvah*.

A unique observation may be the suggestion that anyone who learns Torah should preferably study from texts which he personally owns. For example, two students are studying Talmud. One is utilizing his own volume, and the other, a borrowed text. Since acquiring religious texts is a form of observing the *mitzvah* of writing a *Sefer Torah*, the student studying from his own volume may actually be observing two *mitzvot*: the *mitzvah* of learning Torah, and the *mitzvah* of writing a *Sefer Torah*. Further attention should be directed to this question.

This consideration may not be applicable to religious texts owned by a synagogue or a communal institution. The *Magen Avraham* rules that just as a community is mandated to acquire a *Sefer Torah*, *Nevi'im*, and *Ketuvin*, so too is it obliged to acquire a Talmud (*Orach Chayyim* 150:1). Perhaps a condition of a communal text is that whoever utilizes it is granted ownership during the process. As a result, for each individual, the community is facilitating not only the means of learning Torah but also the *mitzvah* of writing a *Sefer Torah*, which is fulfilled by learning in a personally owned text.

16

Analysis of the Theory of the Lubavitcher Rebbe, *Shlita*

It should be noted that those who subscribe to the customs of Chabad manifest a unique orientation to the *mitzvah* of writing a *Sefer Torah*. The Rebbe (see *Hitvadut*, 19 Kislev 5742, *Bilti Mugah*) ponders the problem of why the *mitzvah* of writing a *Sefer Torah* is rarely performed. Incredible as it seems, even great Chasidic Rebbes who cherished the performance of *mitzvot* hardly ever involved themselves in the process of writing a *Sefer Torah*. Indeed, even those who did observe the *mitzvah* wrote their *Sifrei Torah* at advanced ages and not at their Bar Mitzvah. Why?

The Rebbe presents a unique analysis of the role of a communal *Sefer Torah*. He suggests that every communal *Sefer Torah* has a conditional aspect to it—namely, it is acquired on the condition that ownership is granted to each person who utilizes it (*layv bet din matna*). Thus, each person called to the Torah for an *aliyah* is vested with total ownership of the *Sefer Torah*. The *berachah* is a public form of personal testimony that the *Sefer Torah* is kosher; for, of course, no blessing may be chanted over an invalid *Sefer Torah*. This means that upon receiving an *aliyah* to the Torah, one simultaneously may acquire the *mitzvah* of learning in a personal *Sefer Torah*, which is the purpose of the *mitzvah* of writing a *Sefer Torah*. For this reason, also, a Bar Mitzvah boy celebrates his new status by being called to the

Torah. In other words, every Jew acquires the *mitzvah* of writing a *Sefer Torah* in some form every time he is called for an *aliyah* to the Torah.

The precedent for this analysis is the communal *etrog* utilized in many communities. As is well known, one must personally own an *etrog* in order to properly observe the *mitzvah (lachem)*. Nonetheless, many communities utilize a communal *etrog*, vesting each user of the *etrog*, in turn, with total ownership of the *etrog* at the moment of performing the *mitzvah*. Just as the user's personal ownership terminates upon conclusion of the *mitzvah*, so too with the *Sefer Torah* (ibid., pp. 22–28).

A preliminary assumption, based solely upon the preceding presentation, is that the Rebbe holds the position that continued ownership of a *Sefer Torah* has no relevance to the performance of the *mitzvah* of writing a *Sefer Torah*. The basis for this assumption is the policy that each person who obtains an *aliyah* is vested with the *mitzvah* of writing a *Sefer Torah*. Yet, according to the Rebbe, ownership terminates at the conclusion of the *aliyah* and is then vested to the next person who receives an *aliyah*. If loss of ownership is a factor which annuls the *mitzvah*, then at the conclusion of each *aliyah*, whatever *mitzvah* was gained would be lost. Thus, retaining ownership in a *Sefer Torah* granted to a synagogue, to sustain permanent possession, would suggest a Halachic practice contrary to the Rebbe's position. Indeed, the donor's retention of ownership would withhold from anyone who received an *aliyah* the right to own the *Sefer Torah* while chanting the *berachah*, and this would negate the very essence of the principle. As a result, the community might not wish to utilize such a *Sefer Torah* for regular public readings. Thus, retaining ownership may detract from the *Sefer Torah* and deny other Jews the opportunity to perform the Biblical *mitzvah*.

In subsequent discourses (see *Hitvadot, Parashat Vayeshev, 5742, Bilti Mugah*; also *Hitvadut, Layl* 2 Chanukah 5742, *Bilti Mugah*), the Rebbe clarified and expanded his position. The pertinent concepts are:

1. In general, a communal *Sefer Torah* is written expressly in behalf of a community. As a result, the communal factor is present at the inception of the *Sefer Torah*. Thus, the *Sefer Torah* was instituted with the condition that each person is vested with ownership at the moment of his *aliyah* (*layv bet din matna*). It is in this circumstance that the above principle is noted and not in a case of a person writing a *Sefer Torah* expressly for himself and subsequently donating it to a synagogue (*Vayeshev*, p. 14).

2. Each person who receives an *aliyah* manifests the three basic aspects of the *mitzvah*: (a) as a member of the community, it is considered as if he wrote the *Sefer Torah* himself; (b) he has ownership; (c) as he reads in the Torah he observes the *mitzvah* of learning in his own *Sefer Torah* (ibid., p. 15).

3. The *sofer* is the agent (*shaliach*) of the community. Obviously it is impossible for him to be the agent of people who are not yet alive. Whenever the *Sefer Torah* is checked and corrected, the *sofer* takes on the status of an agent for those who were born since the original writing or since the last periodic check, thus enabling them to be vested with ownership whenever they have *aliyot* thereafter (ibid., p. 15).

4. The *mitzvah* of writing a *Sefer Torah* has two essential elements: (a) the act of writing, and (b) the status of ownership. Those who maintain that the purchase of a *Sefer Torah* vests the buyer with the *mitzvah* consider the act of purchase comparable to the act of writing. Those who disagree maintain that the act of writing is necessary to the *mitzvah* and no other act is comparable. In consequence, an heir who inherits a *Sefer Torah* is not vested with the *mitzvah*, for acquiring it did not require any action on his part (ibid., p. 16).

5. Even those who invalidate the writing of a *Sefer Torah* through the medium of a partnership would permit a partnership situation where it was a condition that each partner is vested with total ownership at the moment that he uses or learns from the *Sefer Torah*. The insistence upon a personal *Sefer Torah* is to ensure ownership and observance. In a partnership where vesting is voluntary, it is possible that the

mitzvah may not be observed, for the process of vesting ownership may not be properly provided or extended. The same holds true when an individual donates a *Sefer Torah* to a community, for the *Sefer Torah* may not be granted properly to the community. The utilization of a *Sefer Torah* expressly written for a community forestalls such problems. This may be clarified by reviewing the earlier discussion of an *etrog*. A communal *etrog* is acquired on the condition that each person owns it at the moment of use. There is no question pertaining to the vesting of ownership. A person who provides an *etrog* for communal use must stipulate to each user that the *etrog* is granted on the condition that it is a present and must subsequently be returned. A communal *etrog* does not need such specific conditions. It is understood that ownership is vested. So too, with a communal *Sefer Torah* (ibid., pp. 16–17).

6. Continued ownership of a *Sefer Torah* is necessary only at the moment of the observance of the *mitzvah*—i.e., when it is used for purposes of Torah study. Ownership is not necessary, for example, when one is eating, drinking, or praying. Thus it is proper for ownership in a communal *Sefer Torah* to be vested at the moment of the *aliyah*, for that is when it is necessary (ibid., p. 17).

7. A person who sells or loses a *Sefer Torah* may lose the *mitzvah*. Not having his personal *Sefer Torah*, he is not able to use it as a text for study, but he can certainly observe the *mitzvah* by utilizing the communal *Sefer Torah* (*Chanukah*, p. 12).

It is interesting to note that the *Minchat Chinnuch* (*mitzvah* 613) anticipates some of the Rebbe's questions pertaining to the *mitzvah* of writing a *Sefer Torah*. He states that there is no custom at all to observe the *mitzvah* of writing a *Sefer Torah* when a boy attains the age of Bar Mitzvah. Indeed, he also suggests that each person who reads in the Torah may possibly acquire total possession of the *Sefer Torah*—a theory quite comparable to the Rebbe's concept. Yet the *Minchat Chinnuch* does not attach great importance to this position, for he contends that one may not observe the *mitzvah* by acquiring a *Sefer Torah* by means of purchase. His ruling is based upon the Rambam, who does not mention at all that the *mitzvah* may be observed by a purchase. Also, he contends that there is no logical distinction between an inheritance and a purchase. Just as one cannot observe the *mitzvah* through the vehicle of an inheritance, so too the *mitzvah* cannot be fulfilled by means of a purchase.

Indeed, it may be stated that the Rambam cannot be utilized as a source to invalidate the *mitzvah* of a *Sefer Torah* obtained through a purchase. R. Meir Cohen, *z.l.*, my saintly, scholarly, and well-loved father (*Chelkat Meir*, vol. 1, p. 16), noted that the Rambam, in his *Sefer HaMitzvot* (18), clearly stated that one may observe the *mitzvah* by buying a *Sefer Torah*. (See also *Beit Halevi* [*Responsa*, vol. 1, no. 6], who theoretically and logically developed a position comparable to that of the *Minchat Chinnuch* but noted that the *Sefer HaMitzvot* clearly disputed the position.)

Indeed, the Rebbe does delineate a distinction between inheriting and buying a *Sefer Torah*. The *mitzvah* requires an action of personal involvement and effort in order to be properly observed. One who purchases a *Sefer Torah* has expended funds and effort to acquire the *mitzvah* and therefore is vested with the *mitzvah* because of this personal action. An heir does not acquire the *mitzvah* by inheriting a *Sefer Torah* because no action was expended for acquisition (see *Pitchei Teshuvah, Yoreh De'ah* 270, note 3, who also suggested this distinction).

What is not conclusive is the Rebbe's clarification of the debate concerning the validity of a purchase. The Rebbe suggests that the issue hinges on whether the *action* of a *purchase* is comparable to the action of writing the *Sefer Torah*. The Rebbe suggests that the action of purchase may be considered in lieu of the action of writing. Those who invalidate the process of a purchase do not deem it comparable to the requirement of actually writing a *Sefer Torah*. This distinction may not necessarily be substantiated, for it is possible that the debate has no relationship to the issue. The basic concern may be whether ownership is necessary at the time of writing the *Sefer Torah*.

The Bible states, *Kitvu lachem*—"Write for yourselves." The concern is whether Scripture mandates ownership at the time of writing or not. Those who hold that a purchase vests the *mitzvah* maintain that ownership is not necessary at the time that the *Sefer Torah* was written. Thus, there is no concern of equating the action of purchase with the action of writing.

Whatever the issue, the vesting of ownership requires an action. If so, then how does one who receives an *aliyah* acquire the *mitzvah*? What action did he expend? Such a person is no different from one who inherited a *Sefer Torah*. Neither of them expended action in order to transfer ownership. A son who is bequeathed a *Sefer Torah* may use it as a text, and thus is comparable to someone who is called to the Torah and reads from it.

This may be the pivotal reason why the Rebbe contends that his principle is applicable to a communal *Sefer Torah* written explicitly in behalf of a community. In other words, an action was required to vest ownership. To the extent that the members of the community were present during the writing of the *Sefer Torah*, it is deemed as if each of them actually wrote the *Sefer Torah*. Therefore, when such a person subsequently obtains an *aliyah*, he is vested with ownership because of his original presence during the writing of the *Sefer Torah*. Thus, if someone actually, properly, and without reservation donated a *Sefer Torah* to a synagogue, it is questionable whether a person who subsequently obtained an *aliyah* would also be vested with ownership of the *Sefer Torah*, for in such a case no action was expended to transfer ownership.

This may also be the reason why those who were not alive at the time of writing of the *Sefer Torah* cannot be vested with ownership during their subsequent *aliyah* to the Torah. Since they were not alive during the writing process, they were not involved in the action that vested ownership. In other words, the reason for their disqualification is not because of the principle that one cannot be an agent (*shaliach*) for those not alive (see Chapter 3). It is not certain, as the Rebbe contends, that the *sofer* must be an actual agent specifically appointed to his holy task. There is substantial evidence to sustain the view that the writing process needs no formal agent at all (see the discussion in Chapter 3). Indeed, if it were possible to devise a method of Halachically providing the status of an action to anyone who received an *aliyah* to the Torah, then children who were not alive during the writing process would still be vested with ownership even in a *Sefer Torah* that had never been corrected. The Rebbe alludes to the fact that an individual who writes a personal *Sefer Torah* and then donates it to a synagogue may, if the conditions are totally proper, vest others with ownership when they receive an *aliyah*. He discounts such a possibility by questioning whether such an act would be properly implemented, but in such a circumstance, the individuals would not have performed an action necessary to vest the ownership

The example of the fine distinction between a communal *etrog* and one provided for communal use by an individual does not accurately articulate the total situation pertaining to a *Sefer Torah*. Indeed, it glaringly neglects a third important consideration. A communal *etrog* may be accquired in one of three ways:

1. It is originally purchased for communal purposes.
2. An individual acquires an *etrog* and provides the community with the opportunity to use it but retains individual ownership.
3. An individual purchases an *etrog* for himself and then grants it to the community, providing the community with total ownership.

The Rebbe relates only to the first two examples and not to the third. Is it not obvious that once a personal *etrog* is totally granted to the community, without any retention of ownership, the case is wholly comparable to an *etrog* originally acquired for communal purposes? If so, then a *Sefer Torah* of an individual which was subsequently totally donated to a synagogue would be comparable to a *Sefer Torah* expressly written for a community. In such a situation there would be no concern over the type of voluntary, discretional control by the donor each time the *Sefer Torah* was utilized. Once the *Sefer Torah* is formally donated to the community, the donor no longer has any greater interest of ownership than any other member of the community. The only problem, as previously noted, is the lack of action to transfer ownership when someone receives an *aliyah*.

The Rebbe further suggests that ownership and/or possession of a *Sefer Torah* is required only during the performance of the *mitzvah*. It is not a necessary factor when the *mitzvah* of learning Torah is not being performed. He contends that someone who loses or sells a *Sefer Torah* loses the *mitzvah*, for no opportunity is available to still perform the *mitzvah*. In other words, it is necessary to retain ownership to sustain the opportunity to perform the *mitzvah*. Thus, the position of the Rebbe may be just the opposite of what was originally suggested: namely, the donation of a *Sefer Torah* to a synagogue without the retention of ownership would invalidate the *mitzvah* of the donor. For even though the donor may, subsequent to the grant, be recognized as a partner in the *Sefer Torah*, there is no Halachic device for transferring ownership solely to him when he receives an *aliyah*. Moreover, as previously detailed, there is no substantiation for the position that continuous ownership is necessary for the observance of the *mitzvah*.

What is of greater concern is the impractical application of the Rebbe's position. The Rebbe was disturbed that hardly anyone ever writes a *Sefer Torah*. Even great and pious Chasidic sages hardly ever observe this *mitzvah*. Therefore, he developed a Halachic concept that would demonstrate that the sages and the multitudes actually do observe the mitzvah even without going through the effort of writing a *Sefer Torah*. Yet his theory has application only to a *Sefer Torah* written expressly for a community and to people alive at the time the *Sefer Torah* was written or corrected. Does one have to have been a member of the community when it was written? Are Jews all over the world included within the scope of a specific community? Also, many synagogues attended by *gedolei hador* (acclaimed Torah sages) utilize *Sifrei Torah* donated by individuals, and there is no insistence that only communal *Sifrei Torah* (expressly written for the community) should be utilized. According to the Rebbe, the use of any *Sefer Torah* other than a communal *Sefer Torah* precludes numerous Jews each Shabbat from obtaining the *mitzvah* of writing a *Sefer Torah*. If the Halachah is as presented by the Rebbe, the use of private *Sifrei Torah* on Shabbat should be prohibited.

It is therefore suggested, with modesty, awe, and respect, that the original position of the Rebbe, without the further elaborations and clarifications, should be left intact. That is, that each person who receives an *aliyah* in a *Sefer Torah* totally owned by a synagogue is vested with ownership of the *Sefer Torah*. This is the very condition by which a synagogue acquires ownership of a *Sefer Torah* (*layv bet din matna*). The problem is, how does the transfer of ownership of a *Sefer Torah* to a synagogue significantly differ from the acquisition of an inheritance?

The Maharil Diskin (*Responsa Kunteres Acharon,* no. 160) rules that the "receipt of a present of a *Sefer Torah* provides to the recipient the *mitzvah* of writing a *Sefer Torah* according to all authorities. Such a case differs from an inheritance, which is an involuntary process." Clarification of this rule is that receiving a present requires an act of acceptance. The recipient must decide whether or not to accept the gift, a process that is deemed an action sufficient to vest ownership. An inheritance is conveyed to the heir automatically. If the heir does not want to accept his inheritance, he must take a positive action to remove it from his ownership. In other words, an heir is deemed the owner of an inheritance unless he does something to remove it from his possession, but a gift which is refused is never categorized as a possession of the recipient. Accordingly, the purchase or receipt of a gift may vest ownership simply because of the effort expended. It has no relationship to whether the action of a purchase is comparable to the action of writing. As a result, the principal theory of the Rebbe now has broad and vast ramifications. All Jews—both those born when the *Sefer Torah* was written and those born after the writing process—are granted a gift of the *Sefer Torah* at the moment they receive an *aliyah*. By chanting the *Berachah* they manifest acceptance of this magnificent gift. *Kelal Yisrael* now has an opportunity to observe this vital *mitzvah*. Indeed, the only restriction is that the *Sefer Torah* should belong to the synagogue. Otherwise, the principle is not applicable. Thus any retention of ownership would invalidate the concept.

An alternative solution is for the donor to retain ultimate ownership but specify in writing or publicly that each person who receives an *aliyah* is specifically granted the ownership of the *Sefer Torah* at the moment of his *aliyah*. Thus, the original position of the Rebbe is sustained as a classic example of being *melammed zechut*—invoking compassionate concern for Jews to properly observe *mitzvot* without disdain or disparagement.

What is exciting about Torah study is that it is a never-ending process of evaluation. It is necessary, therefore, to consistently review basic Torah texts and concepts.

Indeed, when a specific tractate of the Talmud is concluded, the ritual phrase *Hadran Alach* ("We will return to you") is chanted. This is more than a commitment to return again and again to the text just completed. It is a recognition that Torah learning can never be completely mastered. Torah, like life, is not static; new insights will always emerge. It is thus the nature of the Jewish scholar to return to the Torah. In this vein, after the preceding analysis was completed, it was noted that the Lubavitcher Rebbe had published a Torah discourse clarifying his theories pertaining to the *mitzvah* of writing a *Sefer Torah* (*Likutai Sichot, Nitzavim, Vayeylech*, 5742). Indeed, the Rebbe appears to anticipate a number of the Halachic nuances previously noted.

The Rebbe emphasizes that his prime concern is to present a means for Jews to observe the *mitzvah* of writing a *Sefer Torah* under ideal conditions (*Lechatchilah*)—in other words, a process whereby all Halachic authorities (not just a majority or a minority opinion) would concur that the Biblical *mitzvah* is observed. As a result, the model presented by the Rebbe was solely that of a *Sefer Torah* written expressly in behalf of a community. In such a case, it is deemed as if the scribe personally wrote the *Sefer Torah* directly for each member of the community who subsequently uses it (*layv bait din matna*). This procedure (as well as when such a Torah is corrected) grants to all (even visitors) an ownership in the writing process. Each person who reads in the Torah (an *aliyah*) is not considered a partner in the *Sefer Torah* but the sole owner.

Thus, the Rebbe is not precluding other means of vesting individuals with ownership in a *Sefer Torah*. However, while it is possible to theoretically construct a variety of Halachic vehicles for vesting ownership, they may not manifest the stringent details necessary to observe the *mitzvah* under ideal conditions.

For example, the Rama (*Yoreh De'ah* 270) specifically rules that the purchase of a *Sefer Torah* devoid of any corrective action does not grant the Biblical *mitzvah* to the purchaser. The Vilna Gaon disputes this rule (ibid.). The Rebbe, however, refrains from presenting any model that is subject to an Halachic debate. His concern is to explain why historically the masses of Jews did not seek to observe this *mitzvah* with the same zealous devotion manifested to other *mitzvot*. His response was that the communal *Sefer Torah* used for public Torah reading served as the vehicle to vest the *mitzvah*.

Thus, should one be of the Halachic position that ownership is not necessary during the writing process, then even if one buys a *Sefer Torah* and donates it to a synagogue, it is Halachically feasible to assume that each person who receives an *aliyah* is vested with the Biblical *mitzvah*.

Of great interest is the Rebbe's expanded novel view pertaining to continual ownership of a *Sefer Torah*. He suggests that the Halachic requirement of continual ownership and possession was only necessary during the era when the *Sefer Torah* was utilized as a text for study. The logic was that loss of possession curtailed the availability of Torah study. Since in modern times the *Sefer Torah* is utilized only for public Torah readings, it is sufficient to maintain ownership only at such times as one receives an *aliyah*. (Thus, as originally suggested, someone who retained ownership in a *Sefer Torah* given to a synagogue because of a Halachic belief that it is necessary for the performance of the *mitzvah* would be sustaining a custom contrary to the Rebbe's position. As noted, the Rebbe maintains that such a concern is not applicable in modern times.)

The Rebbe, moreover, contends that the concept of utilizing a communal *Sefer Torah* as a means of enabling individuals to observe the *mitzvah* has a historical basis. The Midrash notes that Moshe Rabbenu wrote a *Sefer Torah* for each tribe as well as one to be placed in the Holy Ark (*Midrash Rabbah, Deuteronomy, Parashah 9, Vayeylech*). No reference in the original sources cites any mass attempt of Jews to personally write *Sifrei Torah*. Why? The Midrash set a precedent for future generations that when it is difficult to personally write a *Sefer Torah*, one may rely upon a communal *Sefer Torah* for the observance of the Biblical *mitzvah*. Each *Sefer Torah* written by Moshe Rabbenu was on the condition (*layv bait din matna*) that whoever learned therein would be deemed as if Moshe wrote it specifically for him.

Of concern is the purpose of the original *mitzvah*. If the original *Sifrei Torah* were communal *Sifrei Torah*, then perhaps there never was an obligation to utilize a *Sefer Torah* as a text for personal Torah study. Indeed, this would support the position that the *Sifrei Torah* were originally used only for public Torah readings (see Chapter 2).

One may even theoretically develop a position that would seriously question the general assumption that each Jew is personally mandated to write a *Sefer Torah* for himself.

R. Baruch Epstein notes a variety of *mitzvot* wherein the Talmud specifically stipulates that the obligation is incumbent upon each and every Jew. For example, concerning the *mitzvah* of *lulav* and *etrog*, Scripture states: *Ulekachtem lachem*—"And you shall take for yourselves" (Leviticus 23:40). The Talmud says: "This [process] should be in the hand of every single person" (*Sukkah* 41b). Moreover, regarding the *mitzvah* of counting the *omer*, the Bible says: *Usefartem lachem*—"And you shall count for yourselves" (Leviticus 23:15). The Talmud notes:

"Every person must count" (*Menachot* 65b). Why is it necessary for the Talmud to emphasize the personal obligation? Is it not to be assumed that all Jews individually are required to observe *mitzvot*? The reason, suggests R. Epstein, is that such *mitzvot* are written in the plural construct. As a result, one might erroneously assume that the obligation is solely a function of the *beit din* (as a representative of the community). Indeed, the responsibility to calculate Rosh Chodesh is solely a function of the beit din, for the *mitzvah* is presented in a plural form (see Leviticus 23:2). To obviate such an assumption, the Talmud specifically delineates the personal, individual obligation of the *mitzvot* of *lulav* and *omer*.

The issue is still unclear, for it must be explained why a *mitzvah* expressed in the plural form should obligate individuals? To this R. Epstein counters that Scripture itself provides the response. A careful perusal of the Bible reveals that certain *mitzvot* are repeated in a singular mandate; e.g., such *mitzvot* as *sukkot*, *tzitzit*, *pe'ah*, etc. Indeed, the *mitzvah* of counting the *omer* is reiterated in a singular context (Deuteronomy 16:9). The problem is that the *mitzvah* of *lulav* and *etrog* is not repeated in a singular form. To this it is suggested that since the *mitzvah* of *simcha* ("joy") is appended in the same verse to the *mitzvah* of *lulav* and *etrog* (Leviticus 23:40), all are somehow interrelated. The reiteration of the mandate for *simchah* in a singular context (see Deuteronomy 16:14) suggests that the *mitzvah* of *lulav* and *etrog* are also personal obligations (See R. Baruch Epstein, author of *Torah Temimah*, *Tosefet Berachah*, Leviticus, *Parashat Emor*).

On the basis of this logic, one may seriously question the Halachic assumption that every Jew must write a *Sefer Torah*. The Biblical command states: *Kitvu lachem*—"Write for yourselves" (Deuteronomy 31:19). Since the mandate is in the plural construct and at no time does Scripture reiterate the command in the singular, perhaps the *mitzvah* is solely incumbent upon the community and not the individual. For this reason the Biblical *mitzvah* is observed by utilization of a communal *Sefer Torah*.

The Rebbe conjectures (footnote 51b) that perhaps the ramifications of the *mitzvah* of writing a *Sefer Torah* are interrelated with the Biblical mandate of *velammedah* (teaching it). The verse states: *Kitvu lachem . . . velammedah et B'nai Yisrael*—"Write for yourselves [a *Sefer Torah*] and *teach it* to the children of Israel" (Deuteronomy 31:19). Just as the requirement of *velammedah* is incumbent upon every Jew but public Torah learning is deemed an enhanced format, so too, perhaps, is the *mitzvah* of writing a Sefer Torah an obligation upon all Jews, with a communal *Sefer Torah* considered an elevated status.

This suggested interrelationship may serve as the basis for the assumption that every Jew must personally write a *Sefer Torah*. Even though the mandate to write a *Sefer Torah* is written in the plural construct, the requirement to learn Torah from it is presented in the singular form. As a result, the writing process also assumes the garb of a personal *mitzvah*.

Yet, when the custom of learning Torah is disassociated from the *mitzvah* of writing a *Sefer Torah* (as today), the *mitzvah* perhaps retains its original posture as a communal obligation. Thus, Jews are afforded an opportunity to observe the Biblical mandate by an *aliyah* to the Torah. It is, therefore, no wonder that Jews celebrate a Bar Mitzvah by calling the young boy to the Torah.*

---

*The Vilna Gaon (see *Divrei Eliyahu, Kelallim, Or Torah*) contends that *mitzvot* written in the plural are directives to each individual Jew, and conversely, that *mitzvot* presented in the singular relate to general, communal obligations. Thus, writing a *Sefer Torah* is a personal *mitzvah*, but teaching it may be a communal obligation. R. Meir Simcha contends that the mitzvah (*Kitvu Lachem*) was written in plural form to preclude the assumption that only Moshe was required to write a *Sefer Torah*, (*Or Samayach, Hilchot Sefer Torah*, chap. 7).

Concluding Remarks

As the preceding discourses demonstrate, the *mitzvah* of writing a *Sefer Torah* is not an isolated endeavor but is closely intertwined within the fine fabric of fundamental Jewish beliefs and practices. Its multifunctional purpose is to: (1) facilitate Torah learning; (2) appreciate *kedushah;* (3) simulate the aura of Sinai; (4) teach Torah; (5) preserve the *Mesorah;* and (6) replicate the role of Moshe Rabbenu.

The *mitzvah* of writing a *Sefer Torah* is truly not just another *mitzvah*. It is the concluding *mitzvah* of the 613 Commandments. *Yehi Ratzon.*

As this analysis of the last *mitzvah* in the Torah concludes, may we be granted the *zechut* to learn other *mitzvot* and to return again and again to the teachings of the *Sefer Torah: Lilmod, ulelammed, lishmor, vela'asot.*

Yaakov Simcha ben HaRav
HaGaon R. Meir Cohen (*z.l.*)

Appendix

A. CONSECRATING A SEFER TORAH TO A SYNAGOGUE
A MODEL PROGRAM

Tradition has it that joy on the day the Torah was granted to the Jewish people was considered comparable to the festivities of a wedding. To reenact this aura, numerous customs developed.

1. Amidst song and dance, the *Sefer Torah* covered by a *chuppah* is brought to the synagogue (carried on the right arm).

2. a. The custom in Prague was for the owner or donor of the *Sefer Torah* alone to carry the *Sefer Torah*.

   b. Others contend that *kohanim* and/or *levi'im* should carry the *Sefer Torah*, to simulate the process when King David brought the Holy Ark to the Temple.

   c. Another view is that *kohanim* have a priority in holding the *Sefer Torah* but subsequently the honor may be granted to others.

   d. According to this view, when the *Sefer Torah* is given to a person to be held, it is customary to chant: *Ya'amod Plonei ben Plonei, mechubbad bekavod HaTorah*—"Let stand X the son of Y who is honored to give *kavod* to the Torah."

3. At the entrance to the synagogue: *Minhag A*: A person holding a *Sefer Torah* joins the new *Sefer Torah* and escorts it into the synagogue. *Minhag B*: Three *Sifrei Torah* are held to welcome the new *Sefer Torah*. The three Torahs symbolize *Kadosh, Kadosh, Kadosh; kohanim, levi'im, yisraelim; Torah, Avodah* and *Gemilut Chasadim*.

4. The Torah is brought into the synagogue while all continue to sing and dance.

5. There is a *minhag* to recite the prayers usually chanted when the *Sefer Torah* is publicly read (*Vayehi binsoa*).

6. All the *Sifrei Torah* are removed from the Ark.

7. The *Shema* is chanted.

8. The *Sifrei Torah* encircle the *bima* and the new *Sefer Torah* is opened.

9. Certain letters of the *Sefer Torah* are completed.

10. The donor is called to the Torah and the last portion is read (without a blessing).

11. All chant *Chazak Chazak*, etc.

12. The donor of the *Sefer Torah*, wearing something never worn before, chants the *Shehecheyanu* blessing.

13. The prayer *Yedid Nefesh* is sung.

14. A special prayer is made for the donor of the *Sefer Torah* (and his family).

15. The *shofar* is sounded.

16. A sermon or program ensues.

17. A *Seudat Mitzvah* takes place.

The customs listed above were basically culled from the *Sefer Chinnuch Sefer Torah* by R. Yosef HaKohayn Schwartz, Rav Grosvardin.

B. THE THIRTEENTH SEFER TORAH

R. Yosef Rosen, the Ragashaver Gaon, contends that the thirteenth *Sefer Torah* written by Moshe and placed in the Holy Ark differed from the other *Sifrei Torah* given to each tribe in that it was written *Biketav Ashuri*, contained punctuation (inclusive of the Holy Names), and had cantillation accents. This was the text from which the royal *Sefer Torah* was copied. Each successive king utilized the royal *Sefer Torah* of his predecessor as a model for his personal royal *Sefer Torah*. Such a Torah was stored in the king's *genizah* and used only when the king was required to read publicly *Parashat Hakhayl* (the first day of Sukkot at the conclusion of the *Shemittah* seven-year cycle;

Tzafenat Pane'ach, Commentary on the Rambam, *Mahadura Tenina*, p. 60). Accordingly, the royal *Sefer Torah* was a codex.

Even though no one but the *Kohen Gadol* (and only on Yom Kippur) was permitted to enter the Holy of Holies; *Tosafot* contends that entrance was permitted to assess the status of the *Sefer Torah* therein as well as to correct it should conditions so warrant. Also, from the destruction of the *Mishkan* in Shiloh till the *Beit HaMikdash* was built, it was permitted to remove the *Sefer Torah* from the Holy Ark for review (*Tosafot, Bava Batra* 14a).

Index
Talmudic References

About the Author

Rabbi J. Simcha Cohen, orator and scholar, is the spiritual leader of Congregation Shaarei Tefila in Los Angeles. The scion of eighteen generations of rabbis, Rabbi Cohen is the founder of a national rabbinic think tank and serves at the helm of several national and local rabbinic and communal organizations. His column, *Halachic Questions*, appears in *The Jewish Press*. His writings have been acclaimed as "remarkable achievements" that "succeed in creating genuine Torah excitement" and include *Timely Jewish Questions, Timeless Rabbinic Answers; Intermarriage and Conversion: A Halachic Solution; The Jewish Heart;* and *How Does Jewish Law Work?: A Rabbi Analyzes 95 Contemporary Halachic Questions.*